Sexual Maturity for Women

Sexual Maturity for Women

Mary Deatrick

VISION HOUSE PUBLISHERS
SANTA ANA, CALIFORNIA 92705

Sexual Maturity for Women

Copyright © 1976 by Vision House Publishers
Santa Ana, California 91705
Library of Congress Catalog Card No. 76-40715
ISBN 0-88449-058-0

Printed in the United States of America.

Dedicated to . . .

Sue Townsend, who recognized the need,
prayed for a teacher,
and would not allow me to ignore God's call . .
Ruth Hanson, for cartoons that tell it better . . .
Sandy Keith, for her editing expertise . . .
Mama, for loving and praying . . .
Bill, for being just what I need . . .

and . . .

To God be the glory!

 Contents

FOREWORD

This book is for all the women I have known who have had or ever will have problems in their marriage. It is for all those who have honored me by pouring out their heart and sharing their most intimate feelings, fears, and frustrations. It is for those with whom I have wept and prayed, for those with whom I have rejoiced and laughed.

Never, in the beginnings, could I have imagined where God had destined this ministry to go, for my heart has always been with the individual and not the masses. Even now, when I speak to hundreds at a time, I am still aware of the single faces.

"Who is weak without my being weak? Who is led into sin without my intense concern?" "... If one member suffers, all the members suffer with it; if one member is honored, all the members rejoice with it" (2 Corinthians 11:29; 1 Corinthians 12:26).

Behind many smiling faces is a great ache and "howling wilderness" that needs the touch of compassion and love. It is my prayer that in some way this book will relieve a small portion of those pains.

Mary Rae Deatrick
San Diego, California

There I am staring back at me from the mirror. Good grief! What's happened? I look different than I remembered. Maybe I'm seeing myself—really seeing—for the first time. Is it going to be worth all the effort? Can all of those terrific things be achieved in me? Maybe I'll wait until tomorrow to begin. I don't want to rush into things. After all, I need to think about it. Tomorrow will be soon enough. Yes, I'll start tomorrow. But... then again, if I really put my mind and heart into it....

 CHAPTER 1

Listen to the Lord

God has a great deal to tell women in the area of sexual maturity, but sadly a great many of us have not been listening, so we're finding ourselves in trouble in our homes and with our husbands. In this book I will be presenting some truths to you that'll make you say, "Good! Now it's confirmed in my own heart—someone else is saying what I've been thinking all these years." You'll feel good about that! Some things will be new to you, and you'll ponder them in your heart. The Holy Spirit will teach you, dividing right from wrong for you so that you will know how to proceed in your own home and with your own husband.

This study is an accumulation of my own personal experience as well as that of other teachers and authors, but the study was really born while I was counseling numerous women. Most of the time when we got down to the crux of their problem, it turned out to be their sexual relationship with their husbands. Rather than saying, "Well, I believe . . ." I began digging into Scripture so that I could say to women in trouble, "Thus saith the

Lord. . . ." Instead of just being *my* opinion, my words would be what *the Father* says, and that carries a lot of weight!

Absolutely Irreconcilable?

After I started counseling women with "Thus saith the Lord," I began to see some wonderful things happen. Problems that were "absolutely irreconcilable" were resolved, and as women began walking in the truth of God, they saw Him doing amazing things in their homes. Now I know that God can still do miracles today! If we will open ourselves up today, we will find miracles of love happening to all of us. I don't claim to have all the answers, but I do have part of the truth. It's like breaking bread—you get part of the bread here and part of the bread there, and pretty soon you have a whole loaf. So take the bread that's nourishing to you today and combine it with some other bread that you have, and you'll come up with a nice, nourishing meal for yourself and your family.

I've been married for 24 years, and during some of those years it was a struggle, simply because I'm not perfect. But after 24 years I *do* have some idea of both the things that work and the things that don't work, and I have had to learn a lot of things the hard way. My husband is five years older than I, and he is a very gentle and patient man, but he is also very firm. He had to do a lot of waiting while I just plain grew up, so he has a lot of scars. But we do have something going now, and it's something good. I only wish I had discovered this earlier.

The Spark Plug of Marriage

If a mechanic came to you today with a daylong seminar on spark plugs, and he spent six hours teaching you about the function of spark plugs and how they work in the whole setup of the car, you wouldn't go away saying, "What a dumb mechanic; all he knows about is spark plugs!" You would realize that he knew about other things in the car that made it go, and that there were various functions of the different parts of the car.

Please remember that as you study this book. We are teaching about sex in marriage and how the Lord looks at this, but don't make the mistake of assuming that this is all there is to marriage. I realize that there are other important things that go into establishing a good foundation in marriage. But you do need spark plugs to make a car go. That's what I think of the sexual relationship—it's the spark plug of marriage.

The whole purpose of this book is to bring you into the God-given freedom of the sex relationship with your husband. I have found that Satan has truly robbed women of the joy and fulfillment that the Father intended for them to have in marriage, and that in this particular area of marriage Satan is an especially vicious thief. So let's get mad at the enemy and determine to learn what we can. Let's see what God has provided for us, so that we can walk in the fullness of that joy which delights His heart and ours.

Give the Call to Freedom!

About two years ago another Bible teacher and I suddenly realized that the field was ripe for harvest, and that we were to give the call to freedom! We've been doing just that, and are now seeing the fruit of that freedom. I can't tell you how it thrills my heart to see God anoint His truth. Truly the field is ripe for harvest. Recently a dear woman wrote to me, "Our lives have been changed dramatically just because of your teachings and the books you have recommended. We are both so much happier. We want to thank you, Mary, but I must remain anonymous." At the very bottom of the note, in a different hand and different ink, were the words, "Amen from the husband." One husband wanted to send me roses, but he thought this might be misunderstood, so he just sent me a little note instead! I often get funny looks when I'm standing around church. I'll see a couple standing off to one side while I'm talking to someone, and they'll be nudging each other. Then they'll come up and introduce themselves with the words, "I was in your . . . you know" and I always know what class they're talking about! And the husband just stands there and beams.

Another note began this way: "This is a thank you from about fifteen women who are being set free to love as Jesus would have them. Your tapes are a delight and a joy to hear. I've been married fourteen years and have four children, and, believe me, my husband can't figure out what's going on. Praise God!" It really is that way—the husbands are in shock for awhile, and then they begin to really enjoy it. They wait to see if it's going to last.

When they find out it does, they too become enthusiastic about it.

In Hosea 4:6 it says, "My people are destroyed for lack of knowledge, because you have rejected knowledge." So today let there be a prayer from your own heart that you would be open and tender to receive correction, encouragement, and hope from the Lord. You see, none of us has yet achieved perfection, though we're all working toward that end, not only as individuals but in our homes. So let's be open and tender and teachable to the Spirit of God, that He might impart the very truth that He would like to give each of us, truth that will set us free. I can guarantee from my own past experience that if you will be open to God He will give you some keys, so that you can become free after He touches you with His Word of life. Don't allow stubbornness to come in and a spirit of "What can she tell me? She doesn't know what circumstances I'm facing." Even though *I* may not, God does, and He has far better answers than I do. The Father can impart to you words of life that will bring freedom and joy, and you'll wonder what took you so long to find them. I know—I've been through it all.

The Books of Love

Now let me recommend some books that will help you. There are lots of books about sex on the market, and a lot of them are bad books, even some of the Christian ones. I've tried to assemble a variety of books that will help you in different areas. Remember that no one has the whole truth. Learn to be discerning as you read, because then God can impart to you what you need to have for yourself. Remember that someone can come out with an excellent book one time and their next book not be so good. So learn to be discerning as you read.

Joyce Landorf's *The Fragrance of Beauty*, published by SP Publications, is a good book and is fast reading. She also has another recently published work by Revell entitled *Tough and Tender: What Every Woman Wants in Her Man*. This one is for the men, but women will give it a rousing "Amen!" Then there is David Augsburger's *Caring Enough to Confront*, by Regal. This is good, especially when it's in the hands of a good counselor working with you. This book should go along with the one titled "The Mark of the Christian" by Francis Schaeffer (Inter-Varsity). Lloyd Ahlem has put out *Do I Have to Be Me?* (Regal). This is a good book for you readers. Clyde M. Narramore has written *How to Succeed in Family Living* (Regal).

Kenneth and Floy Smith have put out a workbook titled *Learning to Be a Woman* (Inter-Varsity). My daughter first brought this into our home, and it's a good book, kind of a devotional book that you go through and study. I really recommend this one. And Kenneth Smith has come out with *Learning to Be a Man* (Inter-Varsity). These two books are good for your children as they're growing up, especially teenagers. J. Allan Petersen and Elven and Joyce Smith have written a workbook titled *Two Become One* (Family Concern). If you have the relationship with your husband where you have devotions together or study the Word together, this is a good book for you, since it's fun to work together. If you don't have this type of relationship with him yet, get ready! It will come.

If you don't read anything else, at least read Paul Tournier's *To Understand Each Other* (John Knox). This is a most beautiful little book, extremely well-written and such a help. It's written especially for husbands and wives and their understanding of each other, but it will help any of you to come into a better understanding of yourself and others. Charlie Shedd has written *Letters to Karen* (Abingdon) and *Letters to Philip* (Revell). You've probably seen these passed around among your young people a great deal.

Then there's another one for the men, *Do Yourself a Favor: Love Your Wife*, by H. Page Williams (Logos). Inside the front cover it says "For Men Only," but you be sure to sneak a peek at it anyway. You'll love it! He really knows what he's talking about. Now I don't suggest that you buy this and give it to your husband as a present. Don't leave it on the back of the toilet or glued to his bed pillow. Pray about how to get the book to him, so that you don't become obnoxious in your method of approach.

Then of course Marabel Morgan has her best-seller, *The Total Woman* (Revell). Let me quote a little review of her book printed in the Mount Hermon Log, published by Mount Hermon Christian Conference Center: "The author claims that the book is not intended to be an ultimate authority on marriage or to have a ready-to-wear answer to every marriage problem. It offers formulas, advice, and even assignments to the woman who wants to revive romance, reestablish communication, break down barriers, and put sizzle back into her marriage. Some may not enjoy the author's casual, almost cute style. Others might resent some of the advice as silly, or even saucy. But regardless of whether you feel *The Total Woman* provides helpful principles or just 'pat answers' for your marriage, be sure to give it a fair reading."

I thought it was a scream myself. Read *The Total Woman* with the intention of just enjoying it, but perhaps drawing out some of the things in it that would be good for you. I can't picture myself doing some of the exercises that she suggests, but, as I say, learn to be discerning as you read, and just enjoy the book. She has an entire chapter on how she received Christ, and that to be the Total Woman you need to have Jesus as Lord of your life.

Then there's *Sexual Happiness in Marriage*, by Herbert Miles (Zondervan), which is really good. Miles came to write this book as he was counseling some 150 young married couples who were having difficulties. He came to a lot of hard, fast facts quickly, and he's very graphic in the book. I've discovered that there's a great deal that married men and women don't know about the physical facts of sex. Even people who consider themselves very experienced and knowledgeable within the sexual field do not know many physical and emotional facts about themselves or their mates. So this is a good book, and I recommend it to you.

Another fine book is *Sex Is a Parent Affair*, by Letha Scanzoni (Regal). Don't pass this one up, especially if you have children. All the family counselors I have spoken with recommend it highly.

Free Love in Marriage

God does not approve of free love outside marriage. He has not given us that option. God is adamant about this, and I can give you Scripture after Scripture where He speaks of the sanctity of marriage.* Any sex outside marriage He calls fornication and adultery. However, there is something else that He does not approve of, and that's the puritanical approach to the sex relationship. Sadly, I've discovered that this is where many spiritual Christian women are. They're at the extreme of the puritanical approach, and their problem is just as intense as at the extreme of free love, because they are not enjoying what God intended for them to be enjoying. As I said before, Satan is a real robber here. He performs his role as thief, taking from us part of our inheritance that God intended for us to have with the mate He has chosen for us.

I'm going to be generalizing for awhile, so please don't take any one statement that I make and build a whole case around it. Take everything I say in context with the entire teaching. I realize that there are extreme cases, and that some of you are in really hard circumstances. But even though you might be an extreme case, God is the God of the impossible and the God of hope, and He can reach you and your husband where you are. That's God's business. I can't do it, but God can. I also realize that there are areas of responsibility that are your

---

* Proverbs 5:15-20, Hebrews 13:4, 1 Thessalonians 4:3-8, Colossians 3:5, 6, 1 Timothy 1:8-11, 2 Timothy 2:22, 1 Corinthians 6:9-11. There are numerous other Scriptures which refer to adultery, holy living, Christian liberty, etc.

husband's. God makes this very plain. He spends a long time in Scripture telling the husband what his responsibilities are to his wife and his children and the home. But in this book we're talking mostly to the wives. Don't think I've forgotten that the man has a certain responsibility, but let's deal with women for now.

All Ripped Up?

I need to warn you that parts of this book will be hard for you, and you'll feel all ripped up at times. I had one girl tell me at one of my seminars, "I can't stand what you're saying." I put my arm around her and said, "Oh, my dear." She cried, "You're ripping me up something awful. I want to leave, but I wanted to come up and say it to you first." I begged her, "Hang in there with me; please stay with me to the end." So she promised she would. She got up and walked around the room a little when it got rough, but she stuck in there the whole day. Afterward she said, "Oh, I'm so glad I stayed! Will you pray with me now?" And she was ready to receive what God had for her. It was beautiful. It was so sweet.

I know if you're in hurting places, some of this will hurt. But I also know that we have a Comforter, and that He never knocks people down and leaves them lying there. If He gives me a word that falls hard on your heart, He will also give me the words that will bind you up. So stay with me and don't become discouraged.

Whenever I refer to "the one," it's the legally married one that I'm talking about. When I refer to "the man" it's the husband, and when I refer to "the woman" it's the wife. When I refer to "sexual freedom," I'm talking about man and wife together. I find it necessary to say these things because sometimes they're misunderstood. I'm going to be laying a wide, firm foundation so we can build on that. You see, if I try to stuff porterhouse steak down you right now, you won't be able to take it all. First I'm going to fill you with pablum and pureed applesauce and milk, and then your body will be ready to receive some good steak. You might say, "Well, she could have given me that steak right away." But I can't. I have to lay the foundation first, so you will be able to receive the teaching that comes later, the teaching that goes right into the heart of the matter.

Far Above Jewels

Now let's turn to the Bible. Proverbs 31:10 says, "An excellent wife who can find? For her worth is far above jewels." I want you to see what your worth is; I want you to see that your worth is far above jewels. Many years ago I watched the coronation of Queen Elizabeth on television. How regal and majestic she appeared with that splendid crown upon her head! The Bible says that we are more valuable than even the crown jewels. "An excellent wife who can find? For her worth is far above jewels." Now that means an excellent wife in the kitchen, an excellent wife in the nursery, and an excellent wife in the bedroom. In other words, an excellent wife all the way around—"who can find her? Her worth is far above jewels." Now every one of you has that value in the eyes of God. You can have even greater value as you endeavor to walk in the truth that God has for you. Then your husband will indeed rise up and call you blessed. Isn't that wonderful! And your children will do the same.

Proverbs 18:22 says, "He who finds a wife finds a good thing and obtains favor from the Lord." I like that last part: "he obtains favor from the Lord." It's like the Father said, "Good show, boy, you've found a goody there." **God says that he who finds a wife finds a good** thing. Now begin to see the way God is looking at this relationship. You know, husbands are saying over and over (and I personally hear this from the men), "She's a terrific mother, she keeps a wonderful home, she's a good cook, but there's one area where I wish she was freer with me." And you know what that area is. Every time it comes down to their physical relationship together. No question about her value in all the other areas, but with almost a sadness, "I wish that in this one area she were freer with me." I want you to keep this in your mind; you'll see why in a little while.

Proverbs 12:4 says, "An excellent wife is the crown of her husband, but she who shames him is as rottenness to his bones." We have the capacity within ourselves to be the crown or the rottenness. Proverbs 14:1 says, "The wise woman builds her home, but the foolish tears it down with her own hands." Do you know how we tear our home down? Yak, yak, yak. We talk too much! And we can tear down with just a word. So it says, "The wise woman builds her home," and part of the building comes in this "nourishing of the one," by which I mean sexual intercourse.

By Wisdom and Understanding

Now please turn with me to Proverbs 24. Verses 3 and 4 say, "By wisdom a house is built, and by understanding it is established, and by knowledge the rooms are filled with all precious and pleasant riches." Those should be two Scriptures that you commit to memory. I think every woman should have these in her mind. "By wisdom a house is built, and by understanding it is established." You see, there's the building first, and then there's the understanding that establishes it. This is the understanding of all things—in other words, yourself, your mate, your purpose, and your roles: "By knowledge the rooms are filled with all precious and pleasant riches." These are the wonderful intangibles of love, —peace, serenity, comfort, and all those other wonderful benefits of a happy marriage.

Bill and I go to visit a couple up in Chico, and she has indeed filled her rooms with all pleasant riches. You sense it the minute you step into her home. There is a serenity and a calm there that fills every room. Every time we're with them we're tired, since we've either been ministering somewhere or are on our way to minister. Since this couple is located right in the middle of where we're going to or coming from, we use their home to gather strength and refreshment. She knows that and she intends for it to be that way, and it's beautiful. They are the dearest family, and we're always so refreshed when we're there. She feeds us and sees that we're comfortable in a pleasant surrounding. We're not treated like royalty—we're treated like family. Her rooms are filled with all precious and pleasant riches, because she has the wisdom, understanding, and knowledge. She knows what her role is and she's happy in it, and the body of Christ is being blessed by it.

You can have a home like that. You can have a home that people like to enter, and it doesn't even have to be all in order all the time. You can step inside the home and something just greets you there. Put those verses into your heart and mind and memorize them. Ask the Lord by His Holy Spirit to enlighten your heart to the deeper truth and meaning of these words. Let Him teach and guide you into all truth on these verses.

The Wife of Your Youth

Please turn with me to Proverbs 5 as I read from instructions to the men. Verses 18 and 19 say, "Let your fountain be blessed, and rejoice in the wife of your youth. As a loving hind and a graceful doe let her breasts satisfy you at all times; be exhilarated always with her love." That means to be intoxicated in her love. Now these are the instructions to the husbands. See how Father feels about this. There is an exhilaration there, an intoxication of being with one another. I tell you, the longer Bill and I are together, the more intoxicated we become. I mean that sincerely. I'm learning things about him all the time, even though I've known him for over 27 years. This living together and becoming one together is a beautiful process, and I want you to see how Father looks at all of this. "Let your fountain be blessed, and rejoice in the wife of your youth. As a loving hind and a graceful doe let her breasts satisfy you at all times; be exhilarated always with her love." I think that's beautiful, just beautiful.

 CHAPTER 2

True Submission

I want us to look now at true submission. "Oh, good grief! I was wondering when you'd get to that!" The submission teaching and the sexual maturity teaching go hand-in-hand. Until we understand them both we cannot enjoy the freedom that God has for us.

Two extremes have arisen within our society. Notice how clever Satan is. Whenever the Holy Spirit is trying to get a truth across to His church, Satan in his vindictiveness comes up with extremes at either end. At the one extreme is Women's Lib. I agree that it does have some good points. For example, I agree with equal pay for equal work, and that each woman should come to her full capacity as a human being. But most definitely I do not agree with the sexless society that we're headed for. God has made us male and female, and He had very wise reasons for that. He never does anything by chance or whim.

At the other extreme is what I personally call "the doormat philosophy." As Women's Lib began growing, the church in an effort to counteract came up with an in-accurate teaching on submission—a teaching which gave the wife no rights at all, no authority to disagree, no ability to exercise her mind as a competent individual. This false teaching left the wife as useless as a used tea bag—good for nothing, almost a non-person.

Both are in the extreme.

Now let's look at true submission. We want God's glory and balance in this issue. I'm purposely going to quote to you all the Scriptures we women hate. Let's get them all out of way at the beginning.

First Corinthians 11:3 says, "But I want you to understand that Christ is the head of every man, and the man is the head of a woman, and God is the head of Christ." Ephesians 5:21 says, "Be subject to one another in the fear of Christ." When you're talking about sub-mission, would you please start with verse 21, taking that as your beginning and not the next verse as your beginning. "Be subject to one another in the fear of Christ." This is subjection to one another in the body of Christ. You see, being under *one another*, submitting in the love and the fear of Christ to *one another*, is the beginning of the teaching that says, "Wives, be subject to your own husband."

Your Own Husband

Did you underline *own* husband? That's important. You are not subject to what John Doe wants of Jane Doe. You are subject to what *your* husband wants. You are to be subject to your own husband and not every-body else's; you're not the stereotype that everybody else says you're supposed to be. It's your *own* husband that you are subject to. And it says "as to the Lord." As you are subject to your husband and serve Him you are serving the Lord, "for the husband is the head of the wife, as Christ also is the head of the church, He Himself being the Savior of the body" (Ephesians 5:23). Remember, all authority comes from God, and the authority that your husband has is God-given. Now you take that up with Father if you have an argument. The authority has been given him from God.

"As the church is subject to Christ, so also the wives ought to be to their husbands in everything" (Ephesians 5:24). I think it's interesting that Paul says "ought to be." Paul was aware that the women weren't always subject. Life hasn't changed much, has it? This "in everything" is where the ungodly extreme has come in, and I will be dealing with that in a moment. "Husbands, love your wives, just as Christ also loved the church and gave Himself up for her" (Ephesians 5:25). That is a definite act of submission. Christ Himself committed and submitted. "Husbands are to love their wives just as Christ loved the church and gave Himself up for her." He performed a definite act of submission, laying His life on the line for His church.

See how it works both ways: "that he might sanctify her, having cleansed her by the washing of the water with the Word, that He might present to Himself the church in all her glory, having no spot or wrinkle or any such thing, but that she should be holy and blameless. So husbands ought also to love their own wives as their own bodies. He who loves his own wife loves himself, for no one ever hated his own flesh, but nourishes [promotes health and strength] and cherishes it [imparts warmth to it], just as Christ also does the church" (Ephesians 5:26-29). The husband is to impart warmth to his wife, and in so doing he literally imparts strength.

Last summer when I was very ill, I literally drew strength from Bill. He imparted strength to me, spiritual as well as physical; he nourished me. He cared for me just as he would his own body. And that's an act of submission, ladies. So don't think it's all this one-sided thing of you under someone's thumb. Submission is a beautiful place to be, especially as we come into this balance that God intended for us to have in this whole submission thing. When we get this balance, it's not only beautiful but mutually beneficial and wonderful to the marriage relationship and to the body as a whole.

In Word and in Deed

Let's look quickly at Colossians 3. Verse 17 says, "And whatever you do in word or deed, do all in the name of the Lord Jesus, giving thanks through Him to God the Father." That's a good marriage verse, dear one. If you'll put that on your refrigerator or your window as you look out when you do dishes and repeat it several times a day, you'll see that good things begin to happen. All you do in word or deed should be done in the name of the Lord Jesus. It's awfully hard to not keep your tongue under control when you've just said a verse like that! Then it says, "Wives, be subject to your husbands, as is fitting in the Lord. Husbands, love your wives, and do not be embittered against them" (Colossians 3:18, 19). First Peter 2:25—3:1 says, "For you were continually straying like sheep, but now you have returned to the Shepherd and Guardian of your souls. In the same way, you wives, be submissive to your own husbands, so that even if any of them are disobedient to the Word they may be won without a word by the behavior of their wives."

A husband can go only as far as his wife will go with him. Sadly, I have seen some leaders in the church, lay leaders as well as ordained ones, come to crashing halts because wives would not go with them. So see how important your work is, how valuable you are. I want you to see that you're not just the caboose tacked on the end of the train. You're a major part, and it's important that you know what your role is, what your inheritance in Christ is as wives, so that you can enjoy this walk as well as being a major impetus in bringing about godly things in your relationship and ministry that God has for you. And everyone has a ministry, you know, not just the ministers.

Hindered Prayers

First Peter 3:7 says, "You husbands, likewise, live with your wives in an understanding way, as with a weaker vessel, since she is a woman, and grant her honor as a fellow-heir of the grace of life, so that your prayers may not be hindered." Isn't that interesting—prayers are hindered if husbands are not living harmoniously with their wives! Paul has lots of instructions for the men. Unfortunately, when I first began a study of the Word I saw Paul as a rather unbending, not-too-kind man who pointed at me with a long bony finger and said

"Submit!" And I thought "Oh good grief! Oh no!" It was only when I really went into a study of all his letters that I realized the place that, under the inspiration of the Holy Spirit, Paul had put women, and it is an enviable spot. It truly is, ladies.

If you really get into the Word and truly study what Paul said about women and your role as women in life, you'll see that that's the better of the two places. It truly is! When we submit, you see, we're in God's order. When we choose not to submit, we're rejecting God's plan for us—His divine order for us—and we're in opposition to God. Now it scares me to death to find myself in opposition to God. Just because I'm chicken, I decided I'd better find out what my role was, and so I did. And I've come to love Paul. I can hardly wait to see him. He's my favorite apostle. I love the way he has described the role of women and their value, as well as the work that is our privilege.

One Decision-Maker

I want you to see this submitting to one another. God has appointed two board members, the man and the wife, but he has appointed one decision-maker, and that's the husband. Someone has to make the decisions, you see. Now a wise husband will consult his wife and talk with her about things, but the ultimate decision has to rest with someone. Someone has got to make the final decisions, and I like it that way. I want Bill to have to answer at the throne of God. You see, I'm going to say, "It was all his idea! I tried to tell him!" Sometimes he has gone ahead and I have not agreed, but I must admit that my seminar ministry is far better organized with him as my business manager. There are some things where I've said, "Wait a minute, hold it!" And he says, "All right, let's talk about it." So we talk about it, and then I ultimately let him make the decision, and you know, God has really anointed him for this.

You see, God knows what He wants to do with this ministry. He has imparted to Bill the practicality of it while I'm off in the clouds—you know, I just want to teach the Bible while Bill is taking care of the Board of Equalization and the income tax people. "Honey, you're going to have to do this." "Well, I don't see why we have to do it." "The government says you have to do it." So he takes care of it all. Oh, it's a marvelous thing. We're having more fun together. But God has appointed the two board members. Board members discuss things together, confer together. I think of the things that he forgets, and vice versa, and then (hopefully) we prayerfully come up with God's decision as Bill comes with the final word of how we're going to go. So, one decision-maker.

The Head of the Wife

Ephesians 5:23 says, "For the husband is the head of the wife as Christ is the head of the church . . . ." Headship is a positional thing. It is a place, a job. It is not qualitative or earned. The husband is the head of the wife because God says he is. It doesn't matter whether he is doing the things he's supposed to do as head. He is still the head. Notice that God does not qualify that statement with words such as, "now the husband is head of the wife if he is a mature Christian, reads his Bible faithfully, prays diligently, etc." The husband's role is completely positional. If you can see that, perhaps you will be able to relax a little into submitting to him.

Now maybe all of your husbands are superdynamic, spiritual Christians. Yet there may be a chance that one of them isn't! And if that is true, perhaps an understanding of how God looks at headship will help you to be able to submit.

God has given your husband the authority and appointed him as head. And, because he is head, he may if he so chooses delegate some of that authority to you. It is his privilege as the one in charge.

Yet what often happens is this: a wife hears the teachings on submission along with a lengthy list of jobs that are to be strictly the husband's. The speaker, whoever he is, expounds on all kinds of areas that the husband alone is to handle. The eager wife thinks, "Hey, this is terrific," and runs home to share them with her mate.

Zealously dumping the list in her husband's lap, she chatters on excitedly, "Honey, this is the way it's supposed to be. Here are all the things you're going to be doing." His eyes open wide as she goes over the list item-by-item and finishes by ceremoniously dumping the checkbook in his lap.

So he writes out a couple of checks, and the money is gone. She says, "Why did you do it that way? You're supposed to pay a little to this one and a little to that one." "Well, I just paid the bills until the money was gone." "But that isn't the way you're supposed to do it." "How should I know? You've always taken care of it. I just did what you told me." You see, sometimes we dump things into their laps that they're not ready to do, or perhaps they just don't want to do.

Though Bill and I always discuss expenses together, I am the one who writes the checks. "Paying the bills" is my job. Now you might think that's wrong, but my husband prefers it that way. He simply doesn't want the hassle of writing and balancing, so he has delegated that job to me. You see, be obedient to your own husband. Much of what you will be doing will be because he delegated you the authority to do it. Don't take the model of someone else. Don't try to shove him into someone's stereotype of what all men are supposed to do. God is not in the business of producing robots and stereotyped people. We're all different.

Just the Opposite

There is one couple that has the most delicious marriage going. They are just the opposite of what you think they should be. She is the one who is the college graduate and she is the one who put him through trade school. She is the one who helped him become established in the trade that he is operating in now. She is the one who handles the money. He absolutely adores her, and she thinks he is the greatest thing on two legs. And they have the best marriage going.

Yet this is just the opposite of what we think it should be. You see, I want you to get this balance of submission correct. All men do not have to handle all the checks and balance the checkbook. This doesn't make an ungodly marriage, nor does it make the husband less masculine for not performing a stereotyped role. You might have a better head for business than he does, so that's why God gave you to him. He knew that you would keep the money wisely. If He had put two spend-thrifts together, you would never have made it. You see how God balances a marriage. Yet often in our zeal to become the "godly wife" we run home from the seminar, throw the checkbook at our husband, and say matter-of-factly, "Here, this is your job," leaving the husband utterly confused and sometimes hurt and angry. We haven't proved a thing.

Some women cannot be trusted and 'run amuck' with the charge plate or check book.

Yet I know that this approach does sometimes work. There are some wives who cannot be trusted with a checkbook or a charge card, who gleefully run amuck, pen stuck behind her ear, packages hanging from every finger, and little Johnny clutching the only available spot left, the back of her leg. When those wives "hear" and race home from the seminar to hand over their passports to poverty, the grateful husband says, "Thank goodness, I'm glad it finally got through," and he takes over.

Some of us are so dominant that if our husband tries to perform a headship role we fight him for it. Decide, with the Holy Spirit helping you, what it is that your husband desires of you, what it is that he wants to delegate to you, what it is that he does not want you to be handling, and then be obedient to him. If you once get that balance squared away you're going to be a lot happier. God never intended for all of you to be exactly alike. He said to be obedient to your *own husband*. For each of you, your husband is head over you and Christ is his head, and He'll make a beautiful balance together.

Spiritual Headship

Now for the second principle—*spiritual* headship. Some women who have heard extreme submission teaching on the wrong end have refused to take any initiative in the spiritual rearing of their children because they are waiting for their husband to take over as spiritual head. That's a cop-out. There are all kinds of Biblical instructions to parents showing that you are equally responsible before God in the spiritual rearing of your children. Daddy's responsible too, but Proverbs 1:8

says, "Hear my son, your Father's instructions, and do not forsake your mother's teaching." Proverbs 6:20 says, "Observe the commandment of your father and do not forsake the teaching of your mother." In 2 Timothy 1:5 Paul tells Timothy that he recognized the faith that first dwelt in his grandmother, Lois, and in his mother, Eunice, and then he adds, "I see the same faith functioning in you." You see, the women play a major role in the spiritual rearing of their children.

Instructions to parents are given in Deuteronomy chapters 4, 6, and 11, and Proverbs 22:6 says, "Train up a child in the way he should go." Those are instructions to parents, both husband and wife. In Deuteronomy 31:12 Moses said, "Assemble the people, the men and the women and the children . . . in order that they may hear and learn and fear the Lord your God." Joshua 8:35 adds, "There was not a word of all that Moses had commanded which Joshua did not read before all the assembly of Israel, with the women and the little ones and the strangers who were living among them." So you can see that Biblical instructions are given to men and women, parents together.

Don't wait for your husband to become the spiritual head of the family if he is unsaved or "unspiritual." Don't wait for him to pray with little Johnny or to read Scripture with little Johnny or whatever. With one couple I know, the husband was the head and she knew that, and it was a beautiful relationship, even though he was not yet saved. Every night she would pray with her little daughter. Then she began taking her husband by the hand, and they would go in and kneel together, and she would pray as the two of them knelt together with the little girl. She would thank Father for the day and ask Jesus to care for her through the night and so forth. Do you know what that little girl is going to remember? Mommy and Daddy always prayed with me at night. She's not going to remember that Daddy never prayed. Daddy was there with Mommy. Since that time Daddy has been saved and is beginning to take over as spiritual head, and she is gradually and wisely withdrawing from that headship. Now he assumes roles of leading devotions, praying at the table, and praying with their little daughter. Mommy is stepping out as Daddy steps in. Though she assumed her responsibility when he was not yet the *spiritual* head, she still recognized him as the *natural* head over her.

I Am Unique

God sees you first as whoever you are. He sees me first as Mary and who I am. I am unique before Him. There is no one else like me. And sometimes I wonder if God doesn't say, "Thank goodness, I can only take care of one of you at a time." But I'm unique, you see, and so are you. There are qualities in you that no one else has, and He desires to do things in you that no one else can do in accomplishing a ministry, because He has it planned for you. You have a major role in the body of Christ. Problems? Yes, you've got problems. Made mistakes? Certainly. Perfect from here on? Of course not. But you're still special to God. Praise the Lord!

God sees you as a wife, then as a mother, then in your ministry, whatever it is. The second step to understanding and coming into a right submisssion here is to take stock of yourself. What are your strong points? What are your weak points? One of your weak points may be that you're too dominant in your relationship, and that you're trying to control the marriage. But one of your strong points might be that you have a strong personality, and this might be just exactly what your husband needs, even though he doesn't want you to be dominant.

The third step is to use your strong points constructively. Let them be helps and not hindrances to the relationship in your marriage (or any relationship in the body of Christ). I know one gal who's a good mechanic. She completely rebuilt a Model A from the ground up. Now you might think this is an absolutely, completely male function. But she did a beautiful job. Perhaps you might be a terrific gardener, with a green thumb that would produce envy in the Jolly Green Giant himself. Then husband comes along to cultivate, and there go your zinnia seedlings, the dahlia tubers that were just sprouting, and the begonias you were hoping to enter in the Women's Club. He knows absolutely nothing about gardening. To him everything small looks like a weed, and everything big looks like a plant screaming to be pruned . . . and pruned . . . and pruned . . . .

But, you see, this might be a dominant point of yours that can be helpful to him. Work alongside him, and everyone will say, "Boy, Greg, what a neat yard you have!" And your husband will grin with pleasure, all the while telling how hard the work is. And all the time it was your green thumb that did it. Stand back and smile. You and God know how it really got that way.

The fourth step is to soften those characteristic areas

within our personalities that are most dominant. These areas are not necessarily wrong, nor are they sinful. Yet we must learn to soften their edges so that we can use them without a superior attitude. Don't say, "Bill, I don't know when you're ever going to learn to balance a checkbook." Instead, do what you can do and do it to the glory of God. Be grateful for it and do it without a haughty look, without flaunting and lording it over your mate. If he's not good in the yard, don't say, "Oh, you stupid klutz, you just dug up the begonias!" Instead say, "Oh, my goodness! I should have put these in a better spot. How dumb of me to plant them in the middle of the flower bed and then not tell you where they were!"

That isn't being a hypocrite, that's just being smart. You know your mate, so figure out some way you can help him without the superior attitude of being perfect at something. God intended for you to be good in that area because it makes for a beautiful partnership.

Accept Him as He Is

The fifth thing is to accept your husband as he is and stop trying to shove him into somebody else's mold. Stop trying to make him like somebody else's husband whom you admire. Stop trying to make him like your pastor or your Bible teacher. He is *your* husband, and he too is unique before God. If you begin functioning in your roles and taking these steps the way we're suggesting, you'll find that it'll work out and that you'll be a complement to one another. So don't try to remold him. Just accept him. If somebody tells you, "Oh, your husband shouldn't do that" or "Oh, you shouldn't do that," just reply, "I'll be obedient to him" and watch them squirm! But it will be different with each one of you as you're obedient to your own husband, and you're both going to be much happier—so very much happier.

Number six (and this is probably the most important step you can take), realize that you have the God-given capacity to attract your husband to be the kind of husband he should be for you. That's the kind of husband God intends for him to be, the kind of husband God planned. Isn't that good? I knew a couple where the wife was just aggravating the situation. You could see that if she would just do certain things, they would be so much happier. So we began praying for them, and, lo and behold, she came to me for counseling. I could hardly wait to sit down with her. I gently began sharing with her these practical things that she could do which would help them in their problem that they had together. So she began doing them, and it was a joy to watch him respond to her. He was falling all over himself trying to get to the position to which she was attracting him. It was beautiful. If you'll pray to that end, you'll see it work out. He will soften toward you. It's beautiful.

Three Coverings

Now look with me at 1 Corinthians 11:11, 12: "However, in the Lord [that's what I want you to underline: *in the Lord*] neither is woman independent of man nor is man independent of woman. For as the woman originates from the man, so also the man has his birth through the woman, and all things originate from God." *In the Lord*: that's your key—*in the Lord.*

The submissive way and the authoritarian way should never be carried to an ungodly extreme. The husband and wife are meant by God to be a comfort and blessing to each other. It is God's will that the woman know what her role is with her husband, and it is also God's will that the man not abuse his God-ordained authority and power.

Whenever I speak I have three coverings over me. Now a covering is primarily loving support, guidance, and protection. First I have my husband's covering. I could not teach if he were not part of this ministry. He gives me his covering authority and blessing as I go out. Most of the time he is with me when I go into other churches. He is not in the background. He is a major part of the ministry. You might say, "Well, I never see him." But Bill and I both know our separate roles in this ministry, and even more important than that, God knows.

Then I have my pastor's covering. I tell him where I am going to be and I seek his counsel. He knows where I am and I know he prays for me.

Then, lastly, the third covering is that of the pastor in the church to which I have been invited to conduct a seminar. If I didn't have these three coverings, I could not be teaching. I must be under them. It is part of the submissive way, and even more important than that, it is part of my protection. Those coverings are protecting me, seeing that I don't wander outside God's will. They keep me in His light, and I enjoy being able to counsel with my husband, my pastor, and the pastors at various churches in which I teach. It's not an under-the-thumb, "you can't do anything you want to" feeling. It's a feel-

ing of being free. I'm free to do God's work, and it is a
real joy to my heart.

The Submissive Spirit

While visiting with a pastor's wife one day I discovered taped to her refrigerator door two definition
cards by which she personally patterned her life. To my
regret, I cannot acknowledge the author, though what he
or she had to say was prophetic. One card gave a definition of the submissive spirit, and this sort of rounds out
the whole idea. "A submissive spirit is the freedom to be
creative under the protection of divinely appointed
authority." Does that say it for you?

You see, you are not supposed to be quenched and
squelched as a wife or as a woman. You have a covering,
and it is a protection for you, so that you might be
creative in all those areas in which God intended for you
to be creative, for the benefit not only of your home but
also of the body of Christ.

The other card defined a quiet spirit as "the confidence that God will use even the mistakes of those in
authority over me to achieve his character in me." Now
that one ought to really do it for you! First Peter 3:4
says, "A gentle and quiet spirit . . . is precious in the sight
of God."

Have you ever been in the place where mistakes have
been made by those in authority over you? Just relax
into it. I know that isn't always easy: just a couple of
years ago I myself was in a very difficult situation. But if
you relax into the situation, God will achieve the character of Christ in you and you will truly find the fruit of

Christ developing in you in a sweet, lovely, fragrant way, a way that will be a blessing to those around you. Don't say, "Well, what if he makes a mistake?" If he does, God will correct him and at the same time achieve His character in you.

In the Beginning

Turn with me to Genesis 1:27-31. "And God created man in His own image; in the image of God He created him; male and female [I like that!] He created them. And God blessed them, and God said to them, 'Be fruitful and multiply, and fill the earth and subdue it, and rule over the fish of the sea and over the birds of the sky and over every living thing that moves on the earth.' Then God said, 'Behold, I have given you every plant yielding seed that is on the surface of all the earth, and every tree which has fruit yielding seed; it shall be food for you. And to every beast of the earth and to every bird of the sky and to everything that moves on the earth which has life I have given every green plant for food'; and it was so. And God saw all that He had made, and, behold, it was very good." Now I want you to remember this phrase "It was very good." Don't forget that. Tuck it away, because I'll be coming back to it.

Adam's Helper

Notice that in verse 18 of Genesis chapter 2 God says, "It is not good for the man to be alone; I will make him a helper suitable for him." This helper means another self, another person suitable for the man. Then God goes on to talk about all the birds and the bees: "And out of the ground the Lord God formed every beast of the field and every bird of the sky, and brought them to the man to see what he would call them; and whatever the man called a living creature, that was its name. And the man gave names to all the cattle, and to the birds of the sky, and to every beast of the field. But for Adam there was not found a helper suitable for him" (Genesis 2:19, 20). I believe that God wanted Adam to see that. He said, "I'm going to make a helper for him," and then He proceeded to create all the animals and all the birds. Adam kept looking—cow, horse, butterfly—but nothing that he saw was suitable for him. That is exactly what God wanted him to see. "So the Lord God caused a deep sleep to fall upon the man, and he slept. Then He took one of his ribs and closed up the flesh at that place, and the Lord God fashioned into a woman the rib which he had taken from the man, and brought her to the man" (Genesis 2:21, 22).

This is the most beautiful picture in all of Scripture, I think. The Lord God has fashioned a woman, and now He comes bringing her to Adam. Can you imagine it? God knew that Adam had been looking for a helper, so He fashioned this one for him, and now He can hardly wait to see what Adam will say. And Adam says, "Wow!" That isn't really what it says here, but do you want to know what this actually means when it says, "This is now bone of my bones and flesh of my flesh; she shall be called Woman because she was taken out of Man"? What this literally means in the original language is "This is it."

Have you ever been shopping when a salesgirl comes

up to you and says, "Can I help you with something?" and you say "Oh, I'm not sure, I don't know"? "Well, what are you looking for?" "Well, I don't know, but I'll know it when I see it." Have you ever done that? "I'll know it when I see it." Well, Adam knew it when he saw it. He said, "This is it!" "Father, You're so smart; how did you know? This is exactly what I needed. I didn't even know what I needed, but this is it!"

Gift to Your Husband

That's exactly what God has done with you and your man. He brought you as a gift to him—one more valuable than jewels to that man. And he looked at you and said "Wow!" Verse 24 says, "For this cause a man shall leave his father and his mother and shall cleave to his wife, and they shall become one flesh." If you like to write in your Bible, please write there, "Sex originated in the mind of God." It was not Adam's idea, and it was not even Eve's idea. She had some of her own, but this wasn't one of them! Sex is God's idea. It had its birth in the mind of God. I want you to see and get into your heart the fact that sex is of God and did not originate with either man or woman.

 CHAPTER 3

Leaving and Cleaving

I want to spend a short time on leaving and cleaving, because until you get this into your heart you will find that you cannot fully enjoy your God-given sex relationship with your husband. Are you still cleaving in some way to home ties? Let me give you a definition for "leave": "to depart from with permission and a formal parting." Isn't that interesting? It carries with it the meaning of permission and formal parting. See how important it is to have parental consent as you move into a marriage. Bill said to me one time when one of our daughters had brought someone home, "Honey, what do you do when your daughter gets interested in someone you don't like?" I said, "Maybe you should ask my mother!" (I'm just kidding—she *loves* Bill!) It's so important that we have parental consent as we leave. Now the definition of "cleave" is "to adhere closely, to stick, to cling, to become attached with close and strong attachment."

Let me give you a little illustration. The two palms of your hands put together firmly are like your home tie.

Leaving and Cleaving.

That's the way you are with Mom and Dad. But when you move into marriage, you are to cleave. That's when you get those fingers entwined together and closed tightly. Unfortunately, this is the way some of us have been at home with Mom and Dad, so when it comes time for us to leave and form a marriage relationship of our own, we just can't seem to do it. We say, "Well, we're leaving a little bit and we're cleaving a little bit. There is no such thing. You must *leave and cleave*. You can't cleave a little bit here and cleave a little bit there.

It's like being a little bit pregnant. You're either pregnant or you're not! You've either left home ties or you haven't. Unless you've fully left home ties, you're not cleaving. And if you're not cleaving, you're not enjoying your right relationship with your husband, and you never will.

I cannot emphasize that strongly enough. Begin now with your children, helping them to leave, even if they're little. Begin having a healthy relationship with them, so that as they reach marriageable age they won't come into all kinds of guilt feelings as they begin wanting to leave home. When our oldest daughter, who was still single, moved into her own apartment, it was an emotional time for me, but it was part of the leaving process. She was still under her daddy's covering and remained so until her marriage this last May. Yet during those single years she still came for his advice and counsel. Emotionally she was at the place where she could pull away from us and cleave to the man whom God had ordained for her. We raised her that way. God helped us not to hang on.

Begin Letting Go

Some marriages have the hardest time. I've counseled with so many women whose husbands have still not disattached themselves from Mother. Oh, dear ones, if you have sons, let them become the husband God intends for them to be to the wife He chooses for them. Don't cause them to become so dependent on you. Begin letting them go. This doesn't mean that you will not continue to love them or they you. It doesn't mean that they are to cease honoring you. It simply means that you are allowing them to go when God says, "Here's my gift of a helper to you, that you might form a life separate from your own family."

Oh, so many heartaches. I have counseled many women who have the heartache of being married to a man who has not yet left Mother. So counsel with your kids. Begin helping them to leave. The fundamental law of marriage is to leave and cleave. Notice that God says, "A man shall leave his father and his mother and shall cleave to his wife, and they shall become one flesh" (Genesis 2:24). See the order. Leave, cleave, become one. You'll never get to "become one" until you have gone through leaving and cleaving. Oh, I pray that you take this in and let God speak to your heart. Help your children to become independent people who are strong but still have a loving relationship with you. This doesn't mean that you become cold. It just means that you help them become independent so that they might be able to cleave to another.

Divine Versus Natural

The second thing I want you to see is that the *divine* laws of order are stronger than the *natural* ones. The divine laws are husband and wife cleaving together. The natural laws are mother, father, and children. But God says that His divine laws take precedence over the natural laws, and they always do. God always takes dominance and precedence. If you want the joy, you're going to have to walk in God's good order. Father was the One who brought Eve to Adam. It is Father's gift to the man when He gives the helper, the wife, to him. You are God's gift to that man.

Isn't that exciting? Don't you like being a gift, all wrapped up? God especially chose you for that particular man because for him you are perfect. For somebody else you would not be. For me Bill is perfect, and I am perfect for him. We are perfect for each other. If we were with different people, we would not be. I need the strength that Bill has, plus the force of his personality that would be destructive to a frail, little flower of a woman. I need his firmness. But he has something that captures me, and this something is his gentle spirit. Strength and gentleness just get me, and he's got them both. That's what I needed, and God knew it, so He gave me to Bill. You are God's gift to your husband, and for him you are perfect, truly perfect.

Try to understand the necessity of taking parental consent into marriage. Be praying even now, if you have little ones, for their mates. I've prayed for my girls' mates for years. Bill and I both have. We prayed because we knew they were somewhere. They were already born and walking around, and God was working in them and building them and training them.

I keep a prayer book for my girls' mates. For years, the pages did not have names, only prayers from my heart of the godly qualities which I wanted to see in my future sons-in-law. This last May one of those pages acquired a name, David. Bill and I were truly able to say, "Go with God, establish a home." Raise your sons and your daughters this way even from tiny tots. Raise them so you can let them go with your blessing.

The Closest Union Possible

The Christian husband and wife are joined together by the will and appointment of God in the firmest and closest union possible. Never, never will you find another union like that. God says that this is the closest union possible between man and woman. A man's children are merely parts and pieces of himself, but his wife *is* himself. A man and woman's children are just parts and pieces of them both, but the wife and the husband are one. There's where your priority is, husband and wife. So if you're still clinging to Mother and Father, you're in violation of God's divine order. You're in violation, and He can't bless you in your marriage until you become emotionally disattached from Mother and Father, and that doesn't mean you don't continue to love and honor them. It just means that you attach and cleave emotionally and physically to your husband.

If you have this problem, what are the steps to correcting it? Face the problem honestly. Am I still clinging to Mom? Ow! I know this may hurt. I myself am very close to my mother, but I'm not *clinging* to her. Yet Mom and I are very close, and we have lots of fun together. Square away your own heart. Know that leaving and cleaving is always a heart attitude first, before it's an overt act. So get your heart straightened out, and then your actions from that point on will reflect your heart attitude.

Principle Number One

All right, now we're getting into it. How's that for

laying a foundation? Do you feel like you've got mortar spread all over you? Okay, now for Principle Number One. First I'll give you the short version: "A man's self-acceptance equals his sexual acceptance." Now let me give you the long version: "A man's healthy attitude of his maleness and his conception of himself as a virile man more or less center around how he is received and desired as a lover."

When I first put this teaching together, I sat down with my husband and went through the whole thing with him. I said, "Honey, listen to this principle." (You have to be very careful when you put things into principles.) I said, "Bill, what does this sound like to you?" After I gave the definition to him, he thought awhile, then looked at me and said, "Absolutely."

We have talked with lots of men since, including pastors, doctors, and counselors, and asked them what they thought. Their answer was always the same—"Absolutely." I do wish that women would understand this principle. "A man's healthy attitude of his maleness and his conception of himself as a virile man more or less center around how he is received and desired as a lover."

How do a husband and wife become "one flesh"? Look again at Genesis 2, verses 24 and 25: "For this cause a man shall leave his father and his mother and shall cleave to his wife, and they shall become one flesh. And the man and his wife were both naked and were not ashamed." They were not ashamed before each other and they were not ashamed before God. They became one flesh. How did God determine that they would become one? Have you ever thought about that? You appear before the minister and he says, "I now pronounce you man and wife." But exactly how do we become one? Well, let's be spiritual for a moment and say that we become one by grace. (We always want to throw in the spiritual for those of us who are so spiritual!) We become one by grace, by drawing from the life of Christ. We know that even in the Garden of Eden the life of Christ was functioning, because 2 Timothy 1:9 tells us that we were granted from all eternity the grace and the holy calling that is in Christ. So Christ was there, always there. Even then Adam and Eve were drawing on His life and grace. Okay, the spiritual is out of the way. Now the practical.

How do we become one? By sexual intercourse! We become one in this physical way. Remember what I told you I wanted you to remember? "God saw all that He made and, behold, it was very good." Did God say, "Okay, go ahead, go ahead and do it. Get it over with— quick, quick, I'll cover my eyes!" No, He didn't do that. He saw everything that He had made—every function, every part of it, the whole picture—and He said that all of it was very good. God intended for Adam and Eve to become one together physically by performing together in intercourse. That is "nourishing the one."

What It Means to Know

I want to tell you about the Hebrew verb in the Old Testament which is translated "to know." You see an example of it in Genesis 4:1, where it says of Adam, "Now the man knew his wife." Some modern translations say, "Now the man had relations with his wife." I want to give you the definition of that Hebrew verb "to know" when it's used in this way. It means, first of all, "the sexual love experience that is shared between man and wife," and it carries with it an even deeper meaning. It means "the mutual exchange of the deepest sort of knowledge about the loved one that is communicated during that physical act."*

I want you to get this definition because of how important it is. This verb means that you are exchanging the deepest sort of knowledge about your loved one which is communicated during the physical act of intercourse, when you need to express things that are too deep for utterance, things that are communicated only in the act of intercourse. This is tremendously important. God says that this special kind of knowledge is reserved only for marriage. It is not for extramarital relationships. God intended for this physical relationship to be enjoyed only within marriage, because it is not just an act that "nobody else knows about and it doesn't hurt anybody anyway." With intercourse you are communicating on the deepest sort of level and giving each other information that is meant only for God's ordained mate for you. That's what this word "know" means.

Nourishing the One

We communicate on three levels—body, soul, and spirit. I want to give you a good definition of marriage: "Marriage is an intimate personal union to which a man and woman consent, consummated and continuously

---

* Petersen and Smith, *Two Become One* (Family Concern, 1973), p. 63. Used by permission.

nourished by sexual intercourse and perfected in a lifelong partnership of mutual love and commitment." Do you know where that definition is found? In the *Zondervan Pictorial Bible Dictionary** "Nourishing the one" is built on sexual intercourse. Your marriage is nourished every time you have love together in this way. You are nourishing the one. See how important this is. God saw everything that He had made and planned, and, behold, it was very good. God said, "Terrific!" And all this time you were thinking, "Boy, it just can't be godly because it's so terrific—something must be wrong with sex." No, God said terrific, and then He added, "This is my gift to you, to nourish the one." I want you to see that. This is not Adam and Eve's idea, and it isn't even your idea. It isn't even your husband's idea! "Well, you don't know my husband!" No, it's God's idea! This is what He imparted to you; this is His gift to make you one together, to nourish each other. Don't just throw this aside like it's nothing! God intended for this to be the nourishment, the glow, the building, the edifying process of you becoming one together.

More than anything I want you to see that this physical relationship you have with your husband is not just a sideline to marriage. It's not something you can either participate in or not and say, "Oh well, to heck with it." Intercourse is something ordained of God to nourish your marriage. Just as God has ordained His Word to nourish us in our spiritual life, so too He has

---

* From *The Zondervan Pictorial Bible Dictionary*, edited by Merrill C. Tenney, copyright ©1963 by The Zondervan Publishing House. Used by Permission.

ordained sexual intercourse to nourish our married life. He caused it to be that way. He planned it that way. It is God's gift and it is perfect. God's gifts are always perfect. There is absolutely not one dot of darkness in them.

Satan's Perversion

As with all of God's gifts, Satan comes along and tries to pervert them. But that doesn't negate the beauty and perfection of the original gift given by God. This is what God has done for your marriage. He said, "Here's a gift you're going to enjoy." Why wouldn't He have it so? We sometimes think that when God gives us things that are good for us, they're never enjoyable and we don't like them. No! God has imparted this gift to the married couple so that they might be nourished together and become one, so that they might come into joy and fullness and prosperity together. Spiritually and in every other way they will be a greater blessing to the body of Christ and bring greater glory to God. It always comes back to God. He sees to it that the glory goes back to Him. Since sex is a gift from God, it ought to be wonderful and do much for our marriage. Thank you, Lord, for being so wise, and imparting to us something that can bring such joy and satisfaction!

Once a girl who was about to marry came to me at her bridal shower and said half-disgustedly, "Oh, Mary, I've been talking to some of my girlfriends, and they keep saying, 'Oh, boy, Saturday night!' But, Mary, I just told them that all we want to do is to serve God. We're headed for the mission field and sex is not that important." I smiled at her, "Oh, my dear. Sit down, we have to have a talk." I explained to her that God had ordained intercourse for the nourishing of their marriage, for a closer binding, and that the more they were nourished as one, the more they were welded together, the better they would be able to serve God. How relieved she was to know that she could look forward to her sexual life! She had been afraid to consider that this too was part of God's plan for them.

"Go All the Way!"

As Christians we sometimes think we have to have a kind of superspiritual outlook, but God is very practical. Are any of you familiar with Jay Kesler? He's the president of Youth for Christ International, and he ministers to young people, especially teenagers. He always teaches in these areas of kids and their sex problems, and how we ought to be approaching this as young teenagers. Whenever he has these seminars with the kids they always ask him, "Jay, how far is too far? Is going all the way too far if we really love each other?" And he always very calmly leans out over the platform and says, "By all means go all the way!" And all the kids move forward on their seats and think to themselves, "Oh boy! I'm going to be able to quote Jay Kesler!" But then he adds, "Let me tell you what going all the way is. It's laying down your life for each other. It's real commitment, the guts to have public vows—public commitment, getting that little piece of paper that the world says is not important, committing yourselves to one another legally, spiritually, and in every other way, laying down your life for all time to one another." And by that time they're sorry they ever asked him! That's what going all the way is all about—commitment in every area of your life to one another.

Dr. Mark Lee, President of Simpson College in San Francisco, says the same thing. Speaking at Mount Hermon Christian Conference Center one summer, he told us that when he first met his wife and determined that they were meant for each other, his deep love for her at that moment persuaded him to get that "little piece of paper" which announced a legal marriage. He did it, he continued, so that she would have that "little piece of paper," a reminder of a commitment, just for those times when he didn't love her as much as he did at that moment!

If you're honest, you know you've gone through similar times when you've looked at your husband and thought, "What have I done?" and you wonder if your marriage is all in God's order or not. But, you see, there is a commitment to one another. If you don't have that "little piece of paper" you don't have to work at it. You can just say, "Get out, it's my apartment." But God didn't give us that option. He didn't say that you had the choice of either marrying or simply living together. He said, "This is the way you are to do it. This is the way you will have my blessings." And that is a public, legal marriage. That little piece of paper *is* important. It's important to you and it's important to God.

Becoming One

But how do we become one? We become one in body, soul, and spirit. Please see that each of these parts is important in the eyes of God. One is not more important than the other as we walk this earth. Each part is of equal importance to God. Don't become so spiritual that you're no earthly good.

Now this is what happens. We become one spiritually as we pray and worship together. We have a Bible study together and talk about spiritual things. And as we do this it opens up the soul area. This is where we have our secular discussions, such as, "What are we having for dinner?" "Meatloaf." "Oh, honey, you know I don't like meatloaf." "Well, would you rather have creamed tuna?" "Oh, no!"

So as we work in the spirit together, the soul area opens, which in turn opens the body area, and then we have a good physical relationship too. Isn't that good?

Oh, I can just hear you screaming and hollering. "That's great if you're married to 'Mr. Spiritual,' but I'm not, so what am I supposed to do?"

I agree that after reading what I have just said you may be frustrated and disgusted. What I have done is to relate the ideal. This is how I have been raising my two girls. It is what I want for them. I want them to have this oneness in the spirit before they ever come before the minister to be married. I want them to have that headstart of praying with their fellow and studying the Word together, of sharing spiritual things. That is the ideal.

Working the Other Way

But—what if you're married to a non-Christian or to a not-so-spiritual man? What if you don't pray together and do all these spiritual things together? Are we just sunk then? God says, "I can work the other way, starting with the physical and working up to the spiritual." You have a "body ministry." Is that a little too risqué for you? Well, my dear, you do have a body ministry, and God has equipped you for it. As you surrender to your husband, releasing yourself to him in love and response, the soul area opens. This is where you discuss all those secular things. "What are we having for dinner tonight?" "Meatloaf." "Oh, I love your meatloaf. I even love your creamed tuna!" As the soul area opens up you start talking about things. "How was little Johnny today?" "He was not good." "Well, I'm going to speak to that kid—he can't treat you that way." So there it is. You've opened up the soul area.

Now look at what's beginning to happen. Please don't be in a hurry. Don't say, "Oh, I want him to become a Christian, I've got to get him to church." Just relax. As you take care of your "body ministry" the secular area opens, and then you'll find the spirit area opening too. And because your husband is so content and happy in his relationship with you, he will become vulnerable. To whom? To God.

Barriers start coming down. You stop leaving tracts on the top of the toilet or in his coat pocket (we think we're so subtle!) and you just begin performing your role, surrendering to him in love. Then pretty soon he says, "What time did you say church was?" That's where you say, "Either 8:30 or 11:00." "I think I'll go with you this week." Shock. "Oh, okay." Dear ones, it has happened, and not just once or twice, either. I hear about it all the time. Don't say, "Well, when my husband becomes a Christian, or when he starts going to church with me, or when he finally takes the lead, then I will be . . . ." No, you start where God intends for you to start, by ministering to your husband the way you are, including this body ministry. Then watch this open up your conversation in the secular (I mean in the good sense), and then watch that in turn open up the spiritual together. Oh, it's so sweet how God works! He's so faithful, if we'll just relax and do what He wants us to do.

The Love Covering of the Bedroom

I want to mention what I call "the love covering of the bedroom." Now this, dear ones, is where he will listen to you. Don't run ahead of me—let me give you the proper way of functioning here, because the love covering of the bedroom is something sweet that God has given you. A lot of us are missing this "love covering," which, when used in the proper way, will open sweet times of communication. It's a time when he is particularly open toward you. I used to believe that if all the major areas were going smoothly—you know, finances okay and the kids behaving and everybody's health good—then the sex relationship would be good. But you know, it's the other way around. If you can get the sex relationship functioning the way God would have it, you'll find that it will be filtering into all other areas. You'll find that a oneness has developed that can help you meet problems in finances, problems in the spiritual area, and problems with the kids, simply because you've come into a oneness and communication in this area that brings all other problems you encounter into the area we label solvable.

If you haven't got problems yet, it's because you haven't been married long enough! You'll have them, and you'll have them continually. You won't solve all your problems the first year; you'll continue to have things you have to adjust to and readjust to. But you will find it easier to do as each year rolls on. I can promise you that if you get the sex area right together, it's going to have a fragrance which covers all the other areas.

Now the love covering of the bedroom is this: he's more open to you there because in a sense that is where you are surrendering to him. You can say to him, "Honey, I need to talk to you sometime about such and such." Then leave it right there. Don't say another word. Don't go into a big long seminar at that point. Later you can say, "Remember, I needed to talk to you about such and such." And he'll say, "Oh, yes, I remember." And he recalls that this request was made of him at a time when you were expressing your love to him, and this just swells all kinds of tenderness within him. "Oh, yeah, let's sit down and talk about it, let's take care of it now."

Play by the Rules

But *play by the rules*. I really have to give this caution when I talk about the love covering of the bedroom, because there's always this danger. *Play by the rules.* Don't give sex as a reward or withhold it as a punishment. That's the way the world reacts. In the world, women give sex to get love and men give love to get sex. Don't carry that attitude into your marriage. It is deadly, and it's deadly to the most important part of your marriage as far as your becoming one, the physical relationship together. Approach this with the love-covering approach. When you're all cozied up to him, say, "Honey, I really need to talk to you about such and such sometime." And at a later time remind him of that. He'll recall with great tenderness that you need him and his counsel, and that will attract him. This is another method for attracting him into becoming the kind of husband that God intended for him to be for you. So play by the rules.

What's the Purpose?

What should and can happen during sex relations for both man and wife? Number one is unity—one flesh. We do not mate as animals. We become one as God intended for us to—in a close, personal, spiritual relationship. It's also a practical relationship, so don't try to keep it all on the spiritual level. It's a practical relationship that carries the spiritual side with it. I would like to quote from the *Zondervan Pictorial Bible Dictionary* under the "Sexual fulfillment" section of the "Marriage" entry.

> The exclusive sexual relation between husband and wife points to the exclusive commitment of total responsibility for each other. Sexual intercourse is an act of the whole self, a personal encounter. Spiritually, the act itself must be offered to God in intention and in thanksgiving, husband and wife

acknowledging that God is the author of their love. Sexual intimacy affords husband and wife a medium for mutual disclosures, the senses becoming a channel of communication for all that lies too deep for utterance and yet must somehow be told in order to fulfill the total mutuality of marriage. Such intercourse is pleasurable not merely because there is sensual gratification but because of what it expresses of the joyful oneness of husband and wife. While the sense of independence is diminished, that of individuality is fulfilled. The sexual communion speaks of a pervading possessiveness, each partner offering a precious gift to the other which has been exclusively preserved for that one alone.

The sexual union is sacramental in the sense that it is an outward sign of an inner commitment of love which is recognized as a gift from God. The union is more than physical, for from it emerges a spiritual gift and knowledge. And it is not a mere fact of nature; hence man is not in bondage to it. Rather, sex is a divine gift within a divine vocation, marriage, and as such it is subject to man's freedom and moral responsibility toward God, the Giver. Sexual intercourse is to be employed according to the purpose of the Giver. Such fulfillment is both the need and the right of husband and wife alike (I Cor. 7:4). It must be part of loving the other for what one is in himself, and for what their union means in its exclusiveness and permanence. It is a creative relationship through which a couple express the whole meaning and quality of their marriage.*

Isn't that good? Doesn't that say it all?

---

* From *The Zondervan Pictorial Bible Dictionary*, edited by Merrill C. Tenney, copyright ©1963 by The Zondervan Publishing House. Used by permission.

Grow in Confidence

The second thing that should and can happen during sex relationships is *confidence*: we grow in confidence. We grow in our evaluation and acceptance of ourselves. We bring pleasure to another person, and that's good. (It also causes *us* to be pleased.) The sex relationship also brings peace, for oneness always brings peace. And it brings fulfillment. In other words, you're learning more and more about each other. It's interesting that marriage is the highest fulfillment of friendship. Have you ever thought of that? Are you friends with your husband? I get some surprising answers when I ask women who their best friend is: "Dad, Mom, Sally Jo"—a whole long list, but it usually never occurs to them that their husband should be their best friend, their very best friend.

Let me quote to you something that Ken Poure* says: "If a man and wife were in bed making love, and Jesus Christ Himself walked into the room, He would say, 'My blessings on you, my children.'" Now if that hit you like a slap in the face with a cold washrag, you're not free, you're just not free! If you can't realize in your heart that God says, "My blessings on you, my children," you are bound in your relations with your husband. Very likely your husband hasn't said much about this to you, but he knows you're not free and he's probably hoping that someday you'll come into a freedom with him that will be a blessing to you both. Jesus Himself can walk into your bedroom and say, "My

---

* Ken Poure is the Director of Hume Lake Christian Conference Center, located at Hume Lake, California.

blessings on you, my children." God's gift to you and to the vocation of marriage is the nourishing of the one through sexual intercourse.

Atmosphere of Love

Another thing that wholesome sex relations can do is to present the right kind of family environment for the children. Now don't misunderstand me—I'm not saying that you should leave your bedroom door open. I'm not so liberal in my thinking that I say, "This is the way kids learn." No! You should have a lock on your door, and your intercourse should be a very private thing between the two of you. But, you see, the privacy of that bedroom love will filter out into all the other rooms, and your kids will catch you in little embraces. They should. The girls are always catching Bill and me. They'll walk through the kitchen, and there we are embracing before supper, and they'll say, "Oh good grief, not again!" They're used to that. They're used to seeing us affectionate with each other in this way. They like it. They might make all kinds of jokes about it, but they like it. And they just go on and get what they want from the refrigerator and we continue in our embrace. You see, it creates a good atmosphere for the kids because the bedroom affection filters through the other rooms. You show this affection for each other in many, many ways. Bill has some very cute little love things he does, and the kids get a kick out of it, and it presents the right atmosphere. They see the warmth and affection, the ease with which we show love toward one another.

The love expressed in the bedroom cultivates a loving atmosphere for every family member.

The Comfort of Love

The sex relationship also brings comfort. One year when our oldest daughter was very small, she was seriously ill with what we thought might be spinal meningitis. It turned out that there was something less serious wrong with her, but during that interval when the doctor was waiting to do a spinal tap as well as some other tests, Bill and I were extremely concerned.

Well, do you know what Bill wanted to do? You guessed it. So I submitted. The next day I was talking with my mother (she's so wise) and I said, "Mom, do you know what happened? Do you know what Bill wanted while I was so worried?" But Mom said, "Oh, Honey, don't you see? He needed to be comforted." Turn with me to Genesis 24:63. This is probably the most beautiful love story in all of Scripture, the story of Isaac and Rebecca. There's not much written about it, but can you ever read between the lines! It's a beautiful, beautiful love relationship. Isaac had been very close to his mother, and she had just died. He was now about forty years old and had not yet been married. Now I know there's a deeper spiritual teaching that goes with this story, but right now I want us to look at the people who actually existed during this time.

Verse 63 begins, "And Isaac went out to meditate in the field toward the evening; and he lifted up his eyes and looked, and behold, camels were coming. And Rebekah lifted up her eyes, and when she saw Isaac she dismounted from the camel. And she said to the servant, 'Who is that man walking in the field to meet us?' And the servant said, 'He is my master.' Then she took her veil and covered herself." [This was a symbol of humility and subjection, because Rebekah knew that Isaac was to be her husband.] "And the servant told Isaac all the things that he had done. Then Isaac brought her into his mother Sarah's tent, and he took Rebekah, and she became his wife, and he loved her. Thus Isaac was comforted after his mother's death."

Isn't that beautiful? I was so excited when I found that Scripture. I said, "You're right, Mom, you're so smart." And isn't God smart? You see, He intended it to be that way. Comfort. Does your husband desire this at times when you think, "Good grief!" Comfort is what you're bringing him, and you should.

We have the capacity to put one another back together again.

Putting Him Back Together

Another thing that the sex relationship brings us is reassurance. Ladies, you can literally put him back together again. Maybe he's lost the big business account, his boss has chewed him out, or he's the boss and his employees have been rotten, or they may be on strike—whatever, it's been a rotten day and here he comes trudging in the front door. He's failed in his eyes, but you still think he's terrific. You can literally put him back together again. As far as you're concerned, he's still king of the mountain. Or maybe it's the other way around—you've burned the white sauce, you started to make banana bread but had to turn it into soup, you washed the floor and then the kids spilled Kool-Aid all over it. But your husband comes home and still thinks you're terrific. You're still the best mother, the best wife, and the best lover, and he thinks you're marvelous. You bring reassurance to one another; you literally put one another back together.

By the end of the 1980's, 50 percent of all married adults will have been divorced. Isn't that a shocker? Satan really does have his big guns aimed at the families of America. If he can come between husband and wife, he can wreck the family. When he's wrecked the families, he's gotten to the nation, and when he's gotten to the nation, it falls. The more we can do to bring ourselves into the right relationship with God and with our mates, the more ammunition we have with which to fight Satan. The Lord has His own ways of dealing with the enemy, and He can work best through us when we're strengthened in the Word of life and know our source of power.

CHAPTER 4

The Little Foxes

I have a question for you. Why don't we enjoy the sexual fulfillment in our marriages that God intended for us to have? I would suggest to you Song of Solomon 2:15: "Catch the foxes for us, the little foxes that are ruining the vineyards while our vineyards are in blossom." I suggest to you that you have lots of little foxes rumpling the sheets of your marriage. But now they are no longer little foxes—they've grown into big ones. Until you face these foxes and deal with them, you're not going to have what God intended for you to have in your marriage. Let me suggest a few of these foxes to you.

The Resentful Fox

One fox is resentment. Now I don't know exactly what it is that caused you to become resentful, but you are, and it's a little fox in your marriage. You thought nothing was wrong with it at the time, and that you had every right to be resentful.

The little foxes in the marriage bed.

I have a friend who comes and works in my yard to help Bill and me—in fact, she does the whole yard! (Isn't it great how the body of Christ works together?) One day I was helping her gather snails. She can't bear to step on them or poison them, so instead she takes them home and throws them down her canyon. (I haven't asked her what has happened to her yard from all those snails coming up from the canyon!) As we were gathering snails I found this tiny, tiny little snail. It was the cutest little thing you ever saw. It was no bigger than half my little fingernail, and it had its little neck stuck up with those little feelers on its top. As this tiny thing sat on my finger I said, "Oh, look, isn't he cute?" And we both admired this darling little snail. But then I looked at my friend and saw her holding this big fat papa snail. As I looked back at my cute baby snail and then over at the giant snail again, I thought, "Good grief! This darling little snail is going to grow up to be a big ugly snail and it's going to eat everything in sight!" So cute as it was, I reached over and plopped the little snail into the bag along with the others.

The Staring Foxes

You see, we think these little foxes in our life don't matter, so we just ignore them and hope they'll go away. But they don't. They're so cute and adorable and fuzzy, so we think they're not important at all and that we don't have to do anything about them. But then they grow up into big foxes, and before we know it, there they are staring at us, and we have to meet them. Resentment is one of these foxes, and it leads to a big brother—bitterness.

If you don't deal with resentment when it's resentment, you end up with bitterness, and then you need a spiritual Roto-Rooter to get the bitterness out of your heart. In Hebrews it says, "See to it that . . . no root of bitterness springs up and causes trouble, and by it many be defiled" (Hebrews 12:15). You see, it doesn't hurt just *you*, it hurts many people. So deal with the resentment before it becomes bitterness.

The third thing we have as a little fox is unforgiveness. We just will not forgive. Oh, we say we forgive, but we won't forget it. In 1940 my husband said something or did something and we're not about to forget it. "Oh, I've forgiven him." No, you haven't. You see, you can remember that incident without any sting if you let the Lord Jesus help you. Forgiveness is giving up your right to the debt owed you. It's behaving as if the incident never occurred and the words were never spoken. Don't hang on to any little fox. Let the Lord have it.

Resentment becomes bitterness and defiles many people.

The Sin Fox

Another fox is past sins. For those of you who haven't come to your marriage bed undefiled, who have lived in the world and have carried the sins of your past into your bedroom, may I remind you of the Cross of Jesus. May I remind you of the debt that He paid there. He said when He died—when He was scourged and beaten and reviled—"It is finished." If you've received Christ as your Savior, there's not a single thing you can add to the perfection of that sacrifice. God said, "It is finished." Your debt is paid, and no penance or feeling of guilt will ever pay for the debt of past sin. Jesus did it all. Praise God!

He says you can hold your head high before Him and before your fellowman, because your sin is as far from Him as the east is from the west. Your sin is buried in the deepest ocean, and, like Corrie Ten Boom says, God puts up a sign that says "No fishing!" You can't pull up that sin from the past and say, "Yes, but I did it!" Sure, you did it, but God says, "Debt's Paid!" If you've received Christ as your Savior and asked Him to forgive you, He not only forgives you but He cleanses you from all unrighteousness. That's the best part of all. If you have come to your marriage bed defiled, submit this to God so you can receive His forgiveness and His cleansing. Then move into the good things He wants you to have, and don't carry the dirt from the past into your bedroom. God says it's finished and He's forgotten it. It just amazes me that a sovereign God can forget, but He promises He forgets your confessed sin (Isaiah 43:25). Isn't that great? The one thing God cannot do is to remember confessed sin. He's forgotten it the moment it's confessed. So leave it there. I belabor this point a little because I've found that women often carry this fox of guilt into their marriage bed. Leave it at the Cross of Christ, for that is what God wants you to do.

Premarital Foxes

The fifth little fox is preconceived and preconditioned ideas. Even after years of marriage, you'd be surprised how many women feel that sexual things should be done only in a certain way, at a particular time, and in a particular place. Yet you might be in error. Sometimes that little book *Sexual Happiness in Marriage*, by Herbert Miles, can be a tremendous help because you haven't realized some things that exist as plain, physical facts of the human makeup. So be open to correction of preconceived ideas.

Another fox is bad experiences before marriage in the sexual area. The Cross of Jesus is the only answer to this problem. Bad experiences *after* marriage can also be a bothersome fox. Then there's the fox of bad teaching— listening to the wrong people. For years the pastor of a prominent church in San Diego taught (not only from the pulpit but in premarital counseling sessions) that sex is only for the propagation of children, and that anything outside this is sin. But we have seen the heartbreaking fruit of such teaching. It's an error, and its fruit is rotten, because women come into so many serious problems when they have feelings for their husband that are falsely labeled as lust. It is so important that you receive the *right* teaching, and that you avoid wrong teachers, those who do not have the truth of God. (By the way, that pastor is no longer in the pulpit.)

The Priority Fox

The next little fox is wrong priorities, and I'll tell you what wrong priority I'm talking about. It's putting the kids first. That's not the way it was intended to be. God said *husband first, then children.* You are not building your lifetime relationship with your son or your daughter. Your lifetime relationship is to be with your husband, since someday those kids will no longer be at home, and then what will you have with your husband? You're going to turn and look at each other and say, "Who are you?" You haven't been building anything with your husband during the 18, 20, or 22 years that the kids have been with you, and now they're gone. You should have had those 20-odd years to build a terrific relationship with one another, so that when the kids are finally gone you can honestly say, "Hallelujah!" So don't get your priorities wrong. Now I know when the kids are little it's "Rally round the flag and all hands on deck." It has to be. Mine weren't born 17 and 20 either! They were born little, and I've been through the growing-up stage with them. I know there are things that have to be done at times when they're small. But work hard at keeping the balance correct.

One wife had a husband whose job allowed him to take her with him as he did his rounds throughout the city and into the back country, so sometimes he would drop home and say, "Throw some food into a paper bag and let's go." And she would say, "Oh no, I can't, I've got to do this, and little Johnny needs that," and so on. He's no longer there—they've been separated and finally divorced. He found someone who would pack a picnic lunch and go with him. Later she told me, "Oh, how I wish I could go back to all those times he came home and said, 'Let's go.' Oh, how I wish I had gone!"

Remember who you're building your lifetime

relationship with—not your son or your daughter, but your husband. Get the balance right. You can spend *quality* time with your children. You can spend an hour with them which is just nothing, or you can spend ten minutes with them which is *quality time*. Learn to spend such high-quality time with your kids that they'll know you've really been with them for ten minutes. Then you won't feel guilty when you and your husband go out for dinner. I know one couple who won't go out to dinner alone even though their children are teenagers and perfectly capable of taking care of themselves. So far I haven't been able to convince her that it's *imperative* that she and her husband have time alone together in which they can begin building a relationship. There's big trouble ahead for them. They have not yet passed through their toughest time. So remember your priorities. Keep them straight. Say to yourself over and over again, Who is my lifetime mate? It is not my son, it is not my daughter. I am raising them to leave that they might cleave to another.

The Snobbery Fox

The next little fox is spiritual snobbery. There's a certain phase that women go through—either when we first receive Christ, or else discover the Spirit-filled walk, or else find some other truth of God—that our nose elevates about three inches and we step into a spiritual snobbery level of which we are well aware. We don't like to admit we're aware of it, but we are. And all of a sudden our husbands feel on the outside. Watch it! Watch it especially if you're married to a non-Christian or to someone who is not attending church with you. I don't know what your circumstances are, but be careful. Spiritual snobbery is deadly to your relationship.

I don't want to labor this too much, but I do want to give you an example. We had a couples' Bible study in our home for over a year, and it was a good time together. One of the wives was coming alone for some time, and she and I had privately been praying for her husband, and lo and behold he received Christ. Isn't that wonderful? He came to our meeting and, at prayer time, began to pray in a very childlike way. It was one of the most beautiful prayers I've ever heard, so sweet and so filled with love for God. We were all rejoicing inside at this new babe in Christ. But do you know what happened? His wife was horrified to hear him pray out loud. She later told him how he had embarassed her and that she did not want him to ever do it again. And he came to a crashing halt. Spiritual snobbery. Be careful, dear ones, that you don't find yourselves walking that path and bringing your husband to a halt.

Ask Some Questions

I would also like to add that if you are the wife or husband of a believer in Christ, but you are not a believer yourself, please understand that your mate has discovered a truth that is very meaningful to him. He has stepped not only into *a* truth but *the* truth. His faith in Christ means much to him, and because you love him and he (or she) has this "strange interest," why not check it out for your mate's sake? When you love someone you're interested in everything about your mate. I know he may be obnoxious and pushy at times, causing you to feel irritated and resentful. But with maturity rise above these feelings and find out what this "Christianity" is all about. Perhaps you would find it more comfortable to seek out a third party—a pastor, Bible teacher, etc. You have nothing to lose and everything to gain.

The Fox of Fear and Pain

The next little fox is fear. Fear is a little fox that we need to deal with quickly, especially fear in the area of the physical relationship with our husband. We'll talk about this in more detail later.

Don't make the mistake of thinking that women are the only ones who have fears. Men also have fears and anxieties in the areas of being a good father, being head of the home, being a good lover, etc. Be understanding of your husband and sensitive to his needs for upbuilding. He might never express to you any of his anxieties, so you must encourage his communication with you.

Pain is another little fox. If you have pain during intercourse, be sure to check it out with your doctor. Often there is a very simple correction that your doctor can take care of. Don't put off something like this.

Another little fox is anger. We let anger well up inside us, and then we lash out at the one we love the most. Redirect your anger away from the individual and toward the problem. Allow to rise up within you a righteous indignation for what Satan is trying to rob you of; direct your energies toward *the solving of the problem* and away from your mate. Now these are just a few of the foxes. There are more, but I just want to start your mind rolling into what a little fox is.

Face the foxes and deal with them.

What Must I Do?

Well, what must I do now? We've seen what these little foxes are, so what must I do about them? The first thing is to see and hear what God wants for you and for your husband in this area. Recognize that He wants you to have fullness and joy and satisfaction and pleasure. Understand that *this* is what God wants for you. Next, open yourself up to correction and healing. I was talking with a young married girl who had everything wrong, just everything. Things were such a mess I didn't know where to start. Money was scarce, the kids were sick, and she was having babies too fast. Their physical relationship had gone down the drain because she was having a lot of pain during intercourse and they had not had physical relations for many weeks. They were just a young couple, too. He was a healthy young man, so you can imagine what he was going through.

She said to me, "Oh, Mary, I just want it to be better." I said, "Have you been to a doctor?" Yes, she'd been to a doctor, but there was absolutely no physical reason for the pain. The doctor could find nothing wrong. So I said very boldly, "We're going to pray and ask God to take that pain away, and we're going to believe that He's going to do it." Since her husband worked nights, I said, "Tonight I want you to make his favorite dessert and put it here on the divider bar, and when he comes home you have a note placed right by that dessert, and let that note say, "When you finish your dessert, wake me up." She promised to do what I said, and we prayed that she would have no pain. She called me the next day and said, "Mary, it was wonderful! I didn't have any pain!" She said he came home, read the note and skipped his favorite dessert—didn't even touch it. Whoosh! He came right into the room and woke her up. She told me, "Oh, Mary, it was just like you said!" Thank you, dear God! That was a case of instant healing, and now they have a way to go. But my point is that she opened herself up to correction and healing, and God was able to work.

Be Willing to Begin

God is a sovereign God. He can handle problems that you've had growing for ten or fifteen years, though sometimes it takes Him a little while to create new behavior and response patterns in you and in your husband. Often God will work over a period of time with you, so if something has been growing over a period of years, expect it to take some time to correct. But for heaven's sake open yourself up to healing and correction and get started somewhere. That's the point —be willing to begin. Don't just sit on your hands and say it's too much work, there are too many things wrong, my husband is such a mess, and things will never work out. *Be willing to begin,* and ask God to help you know where to begin.

After one of my seminars I met a woman with some very real problems, so I asked her, "Are you willing to begin somewhere?" "Well, yes, but . . . ." "Are you willing to begin?" "But, you see . . . ." She kept going on and on. I'd come back with "Are you willing to begin here?" but she would always say, "Well, yes, but . . ." so I finally had to leave her. There was nothing I could do to help her because she was not willing to begin. This is crucial—be willing to begin, then start walking with God in some area of your marriage relationship.

Be willing to allow God to lead you step-by-step. The problems that have taken years to grow will not be magically reversed in one night. It may take a week, a month, a year, or sometimes even longer to begin enjoying a fulfilling relationship. But it will come. Once you begin, it will keep getting better and better. If you've got something good going now, it can get better week-by-week. If you've got something great going, praise God and go on to something better yet. God never leaves you at one level—He brings you along more and more, getting you closer and closer all the time. Don't you find this to be true in your Christian walk? You receive Christ on Monday, but you're not perfect on Tuesday. You learn to live and respond as a Christian by putting into practice the things God teaches you daily. It's the same thing in marriage. But you must be willing to begin.

At one of my seminars a young gal sat in the back row with her arms folded the whole day, looking at me with a scowl. Do you think it's easy to teach to a face like that? I kept wanting to look around, to look away from her—you know, to look at someone else who was smiling. I had been told beforehand that her marriage was just riddled with problems, and that her friends had cajoled her to come to the meeting so she might receive words of life. But she would not receive them. The minute it was over, whoosh! She took off and was gone. Unhappy girl! And she was right at the beginning of her marriage. She had her whole life ahead of her with her young man, but she was not willing to receive the words of life. On the other hand, I've talked with women who have been married 25 or 30 years who've said, "Yippee! I wish I'd had this 30 years ago!" Until you are willing to begin, God's hands can't do anything, because you wouldn't be recognizing His workings in your life. But when you're willing you'll just see God's hand all over the place. You'll praise God and take off in all the directions and through all the doors He will open for you. So be willing to begin.

Realize that you and your problems are not unique. Listen, dear ones, I've heard everything. Nothing you could tell me would surprise me. I might gulp a couple of times, but I wouldn't be surprised. Your problems are not unique. You as a person are unique before God, but you never take God by surprise. Isn't that something? He knows it all. Learn to realize this. Know that God not only has the solutions to your problems, but He also has the power and wisdom to impart to you the ability to settle your problems and to bring you into a right marriage relationship with your husband and a right relationship with God.

Be sure to counsel with a competent, godly counselor whenever necessary. Don't tell Sally Jo and Mary Sue and everybody else. If you have problems that need long-term counseling, meet with a godly, competent counselor whom you can trust, and stay with him or her. Don't bounce from counselor to counselor. Stay with one person, so he can help you work through your problems. Very likely you will have to have someone in authority over you before you'll do what he tells you to do. If your pastor is an authority over you he can say, "Now this is what I want you to do; this is what will help—now do it." And you know he's an authority over you, so you say, "I'll do it." So decide on a godly counselor and stick with him.

Look at the Goals

Don't look at your problems too long, but instead look at the goals God has ahead for you. Look at the problems long enough to deal with them and to begin to move on them, but don't look at them so long that they just depress you like a wool blanket over your head. Face the goal that God has set before you—a good, solid marriage. And never give up—it's worth the effort. I have counseled with wives who have fallen on their faces twelve, fifteen, and twenty times over the same thing, and each time I say, "Pick up and go on, it's worth the effort." I know the heartache and the crying and wailing —"It'll never work, it'll never work." Yes, it will work. Don't give up—it *is* worth the effort.

I had one lady say to me, "What if I hadn't done that thing that one last time?" So I said, "Aren't you glad you did?" Now she's got something good rolling, and if that last time she hadn't picked up the pieces, she wouldn't have had it. It was worth the effort. Now don't expect to undo in two minutes what's been two years in the making. Yet your husband will begin to respond almost immediately when you begin to move into the areas that the Lord desires for you. If you walk in the light, he will begin to respond immediately. He may not be saying things that your ears can verbally hear, but your spirit will be recognizing a fluttering of his spirit, and he'll be noticing. Maybe he'll just wait to see if it's going to last, because you've had these kicks before and they didn't amount to anything. So He may wait to see if it's going to last. But he'll begin noticing.

One husband said after several weeks, "Hey, what went on at that meeting you went to?" "Oh, nothing." But the husband replied, "Well, *something* went on at that meeting. You've been different ever since then." She said, "Don't you like it?" He replied, "I love it, but what went on at that meeting? What did she tell you?" You see, he had been noticing for three weeks. Something was different, so he finally asked her. But she still hasn't told him. At this point, I think, she believes ignorance is bliss!

Physically Free

Here's the next important principle: a married woman is not spiritually free before God until she is physically free with her husband. Ouch! A married woman is not spiritually free before God until she is physically free with her husband. Do you know why? Because as you submit to your husband, you're serving the Lord. That's in Colossians chapter 3 and Ephesians chapter 5. We read there that until you come into the place where you have this physical freedom with your husband, you cannot be spiritually free before God. There's always going to be this one area which you're holding off from Him, this one area that you're not allowing God to touch, this one area in which you say, "God, this is something I know You're not interested in, that You never look at, and I'm not going to give it to you." You'll find that growth in this area will parallel your spiritual growth with God. It's so logical that the highest relationship between man and wife, between human beings, would be a blessing to you spiritually and a glory to God. We're so slow to see the practicality of God, of how He moves among us. Yet it is so beautiful when He does.

Learn to Walk

As Charlie Shedd says in his *Letters to Philip*, "Sex in marriage is the twenty-year warmup." This doesn't mean that it doesn't get good until twenty years—it means that sex is a building process that gets better all the time. As you move in it, you learn to walk in it. Sex is a gift of God given to the married couple. As with all His gifts, we have to learn to walk in it. Did you know how to walk as a Christian the minute you received Christ? Did you know how to walk the Spirit-filled life? No. It's a process of learning. That does not negate the gift, for the gift of salvation is perfect. But you have to learn to *walk in it*. It's the same with all of God's gifts, including His gifts of the Spirit. We have to learn to walk in them. The gift is perfect; it's the vessel that isn't too swift! The sex gift is given to unite the two of you, so enjoy learning together.

The Way of Love

Learn to operate in the way of love—God's love for you, God's love for your husband through you, and God's love for you through your husband. Listen to what 1 Corinthians 13:4-7 says in *The Living Bible*: "Love is very patient and kind, never jealous or envious, never boastful or proud, never haughty or selfish or rude. Love does not demand its own way. It is not irritable or touchy. It does not hold grudges and will hardly even notice when others do it wrong." I find that very difficult to read—". . .will hardly even notice when others do it wrong." "It is never glad about injustice, but rejoices whenever truth wins out. If you love someone you will be loyal to him no matter what the cost. You will always believe in him, always expect the best of him, and always stand your ground in defending him."*

---

* *The Living Bible*, Copyright © 1971 by Tyndale House Publishers. Used by permission.

Now I had someone argue with me on this last point. "Do you mean that in any dumb, stupid thing my husband does, I've got to defend him? Even if everybody sees it's a dumb, stupid thing?" Now listen to me carefully. You may not always be able to support the *decision* your husband makes, but you can always support the *man*. Do you see the difference? You might not be able to support his decision. There have been times when I felt Bill was a little too harsh with the kids. But, you see, I was able to support *him* even if I couldn't agree with all of his decisions. So remember that, and he'll know the difference. He'll know that even though you're not in full agreement with his decision, you're still supporting *him*. Be sure to make that distinction.

Love goes on forever, so operate in the way of love. Song of Solomon 8:7 says, "Many waters cannot quench love, nor will rivers overflow it; if a man were to give all the riches of his house for love, it would be utterly despised." Acts 20:35 adds, "It is more blessed to give than to receive." Bring that principle into your marriage and your sex relationship, and you'll find doors opening to you that you never thought possible before.

CHAPTER 5

Men Are Different from Women

Here's something so obvious it's almost ridiculous, yet many of you have never really grasped the implications of it: *men are different from women.* I know you've heard it many times, and I know you've said it yourself, but you don't really believe it. You're still trying to get your husband to think like you, respond like you, speak like you, do the things that you do, and in all ways be like you. But God made you male and female. "Male and female created He them." Let's look at some of the differences between men and women. Now these are generalities that have nothing to do with intelligence. I'm showing you some of the differences that come up, but don't think that every single man and woman fits the description exactly. Yet there are differences between you and your husband, so recognize and appreciate them and say, "Vive la difference!" Some of these descriptions come from Jimmy Moore*, and some of them are my own.

---

* Jimmy Moore is a pastor in Ruston, Louisiana, and is a popular conference speaker. His material is used by permission.

The Emotional Feeler   **The Logical Thinker**

Number one, a woman is an emotional feeler while a man is a logical thinker. You know, men can be so aggravating—they're so logical it drives us nuts. They can have all kinds of problems, but when they go to church and the leader says, "Let's praise the Lord," they respond, "Praise the Lord!" They're just all ready to praise! But women come in and and the leader says, "Let's praise the Lord," and we have difficulty doing it because we're still emotionally caught up in some problem. And that's the way it is. Men are logical, and women are emotional.

For instance, you go to a movie and see Camelot, and that's a very emotional thing, so you're sitting there blubbering. Or you're watching "Brian's Song" on TV and you've gone through sixteen Kleenexes while your husband sits there saying, "Big deal! Big deal!" You see, *you're* the emotional feeler and *he's* the logical thinker. God has imparted to women a certain inner feeling, and we're intuitive about things—"I don't think you ought to do that ... It's just a feeling I have." You see, we women are emotional and intuitive, and God can use that. This makes for a good balance in marriage.

The Logical Thinker   **The Emotional Feeler**

Feeling and Thinking

A woman speaks what she *feels* while a man says what he thinks, and that, ladies, is a big difference. You're expressing what you're feeling while he's expressing what he's thinking. When a woman says "I can't do it" she usually means "I *won't* do it." When a man says "I can't do it" he has decided analytically that he is not capable of doing it because he doesn't have the skills for it or for some other reason. So there's this big difference between men and women. Also, I want to make the point that women usually can't carry a lot inside. We have to be able to get it out. We have to be able to express our feelings verbally because we are incapable of carrying them. We need to talk things out.

Men need to know this. Bill will sit and say, "Uh huh, uh huh" while I'm just raving on. And while he's saying, "uh huh, uh huh," I get it all out and feel fine, and I go on my merry way. How marvelous if we can share our feelings with our husbands!

When a woman hears something said, it is an emotional experience. When a man hears something, it is the receiving of information. Now I want you to remember this because it's important. Words heard by a man are the receiving of information. For instance, your husband comes home and says "Honey, today I was driving on that little street in North Park and this car started to pass me and at the same time this big German shepherd ran out in front of us, and I screeched on my brakes and he screeched on his brakes. And do you know who that guy was driving next to me? It was Joe Blow, the guy who borrowed a hundred dollars from us."

**What a man says is an expression of what he is thinking.
What a woman says is an expression of what she is feeling.**

What are you thinking? "What happened to the dog?" You see, it was an *emotional* experience to you. He lost you the minute he said this dog ran out while one car was passing another—you wanted to know what happened to the dog! You see, what you were hearing was an *emotional experience* in you. With him, it was the receiving of information.

The Personal Attack

Women tend to take everything personally, while men tend to take everything impersonally. Your husband comes home, walks over to the stove where you're stir

Women tend to take everything personally.

ring something, and says, "What's that?" You shoot
back, "What's the matter, don't you like it?" You feel
you've been personally attacked. He says, "What's that I
smell?" You reply, "What do you mean, what's that you
smell?" You feel threatened. Remember now, this can be
important to you. Remember that we women are
threatened by the oblique angle. In other words,
someone doesn't have to come up and be direct with us
in order to attack us. I don't have to come up to you and
say I don't like you—I can come up and say with a quick
raise of an eyebrow, "Oh, where did you buy your
dress?" Immediately you'll think, "Hmmm, she doesn't
think I look good." Oh, the oblique angle threatens us

so! So realize that and be on guard against it. Poor man, all he said was, "What's that I smell?" He most likely thought it smelled wonderful when he came in the front door, and he probably wants to have it again! But you say inside, "Oh no!" You feel all upset and personally attacked. Just the other night I fell into my own trap. Bill said, "What kind of meat is this?" I shot back, "What do you mean? Don't you like it?" So be on guard. Don't always feel threatened and attacked.

Yak! Yak! Yak!

Women are interested in the details and nitty grittys, while men are interested in the gist and generalities, the

Men give the generalities; women give all the details.

principle of the thing. For instance, when he comes home you say, "Hi, honey, how was your day?" "Fine. How was yours?" "Well, I went down to Sears today and I was going to get some lace, you know, to finish that dress I started, and I couldn't find the lace and so I thought, well, I'll just change the pattern, so I looked in Simplicity and they just didn't have the pattern I liked, so I tried McCall's again. McCall's are a little harder to do than Simplicity, but I decided I'd go ahead and get it anyway. Well, then I couldn't find the material, and when I finally found the material, I couldn't find the thread that really matched, so I went back to the original pattern and went down to the other store to see if I could find . . ." and on and on and on. And all he wanted to know was how your day was, either good or bad! Don't give him all the details—just what he wants to know.

Goals and God

In the practical things of life women tend to look at the goals only, while men want to know how to get there. For instance, you say one day, "Honey, I think we ought to knock out this wall and just extend the whole front room clear out there so we can have a whole rumpus room for the kids." Then he replies, "Honey, that wall's holding up the house." But you're not going to be put off with that. You want that wall out! You want the room bigger, so he may come home someday to find you starting the job yourself with a sledgehammer.

However, in spiritual things or intangible things it's just the opposite. Women tend to want to know how to

She wants the room bigger!

get there step-by-step, while men say, "Yeah, that's where I want to be," period. For instance, you've decided you want to have a better marriage, so you start doing all kinds of research. You listen to tapes, you read books, you go to all kinds of seminars taught by ladies on Saturdays! You listen to everything because you want to have a better marriage. You have a step-by-step formula for everything. How do you get your prayers answered? You have a 1-2-3 formula. How do you walk the Spirit-filled life? You have eight steps for that. How do you lead someone to salvation? You've got a formula for every step. Your husband, on the other hand, knows that this is where he wants to be, but he doesn't want you to tell him how to get there. He knows he will arrive there someday, somehow, some way, in his own time. You see, this is how we run into problems in the spiritual area of our marriages. So realize that you have this difference in seeing spiritual and intangible things.

In spiritual matters, women want to know how to get there step-by-step.

The Filing Cabinets

Have you ever heard a man and a woman give directions to the same place? He says, "You go southeast, then you turn north, then you go 3 and 1/10th miles, then you turn east and you're there." She says, "You go

Men are like filing cabinets; women are like computers.

four blocks until you come to the little white picket fence, then you go another six blocks and you'll find that pink house with a bottlebrush tree in the yard and they have a big dog that's always barking—turn right there." If those people ever paint their fence or cut down their bottlebrush tree, you're finished as a direction-giver!

Men are like filing cabinets. They pull open the drawer, drop in the problem, close the drawer, and that takes care of it. Women, on the other hand, are like computers. They just keep going and going and going. For example, you've just had this big harangue together, and there you are tossing in bed while he's out like a light. You're trying to get the thing solved while he's sawing logs all night! Women tend to stew, and this often causes resentment, so be on guard against this.

To a woman, her home is an extension of her personality; to a man his job is an extension of his personality.

To the woman her home is the extension of her personality. That's why you're always fixing it up. That's why you always want new curtains and new paint. You don't feel like you've cleaned house until you've moved the furniture around, because you express yourself in your home. To the man, the extension of his personality is his job. That's why he wants to talk to you about it. That's why he wants to tell you what he does.

About a year ago Bill said to me, "Honey, you don't show very much interest in my job." Well, you see, long ago as we were standing with some friends one day, my husband had said, "Boy, when I leave the office I leave the problems there; when I come home I just want to relax—I don't want to talk about my job." That made me think, "I'm not going to ask him about his job because he wants to leave it at the office." But, you know, he didn't really want it that way with *me*. He wants *me* to ask him how his day went. And so I do. I say, "Hi, honey, how did your day go?" and he says "Oh, good" (the gist, remember?). Sometimes I get a little more information than that, but he wants me to show an interest in him and the things he does.

Get Clear Signals

In order to avoid misunderstandings, be sure to ask your husband to give you clear signals. We women need clear signals on what our mates want us to do, and often we don't get these signals. If you haven't gotten a clear signal from your husband, ask him what it is he wants of you. By doing this you can avoid lots of big harangues.

Let me give you an example that happened to me just a few months ago. Bill often calls me during the afternoon, just to see how my day is going. During the course of the conversation he said something like, "Hey, you know what we should do? We should go out to dinner." I agreed and spent an hour that afternoon giving myself the usual "out-to-dinner" beauty treatment. When Bill walked in the house that evening it was obvious that he had no intention of taking me out to dinner. Because I didn't want to tell him how embarassed and hurt I was and that I had misunderstood his words, I threw something together, all the while pretending that this was the dinner I had planned all along. What had happened? Bill had been projecting

Women need roots to feel secure; men can be nomadic.

A weekend camping trip!

A one-week camping trip!

A two-week camping trip!

ahead to payday. I had immediately grabbed onto a "night out of the kitchen" theory and decided he meant that very evening. Remember, it's *clear signals* we wives need. (All misunderstandings are not this easily corrected!)

Women have a great need for security and roots, while men can be nomadic. When a woman goes camping she takes all her lovely roots with her—you know, a clothesline and clothespins and a portable potty and a pan to wash dishes in. He's ready to go with just his fishing rod and toothbrush. He can be nomadic while you like to have all your roots around you. When you go bye-bye, you take all your roots with you so you can feel secure. There's going to be trouble on that camping trip, I can tell right now!

Women tend to be guilt-prone; men tend to be resentful.

Women tend to be guilt-prone ("What have I done?") while men tend to be resentful ("Why did you do it?"). Now recognize that you have this tendency to be guilt-prone, and face it head-on. Augsburger's *Caring Enough to Confront* is an excellent book which helps you meet your guilt feelings where they are and helps you settle them in a constructive way rather than a destructive way with your partner or yourself. Carrying guilt can be hard, and when a man gets resentful he becomes bitter toward his wife, and the Bible tells him that's a bad position in which to be.

A man is stable and levels off; a woman is always changing.

Laying an Egg

Men tend to level off and be stable, while women are always changing. You're either coming into something or you're going out of something. You're either coming into your period or you're going out of your period. You're either coming into menopause or you're going out of menopause. You're either coming into crisis or going out of crisis, and so there he is, wondering why you can't get it all together. My friend has a way of expressing it: she says, "I think I'm laying my egg now." She recognizes that and marks it on the calendar.

Before I had to have surgery many years ago, Bill would look at the calendar and say, "Uh huh, uh huh." He'd know. Now I don't mean you have to be a slave to your period or to use it as an excuse to be wretched and mean because "It's my time of the month." But many times when women come to me depressed and weeping and don't know what's wrong, I'll say, "How old are you?" Next I'll ask them what time of the month it is, and often they'll say, "I'm just about to have my period." Then they'll think a minute and say, "Oh." You may not always recognize it, but your menstrual cycle does affect your emotions, and when you know this, you can bring some reasonable control to the situation so you don't have to be a slave to it. But it's important to recognize that you're always changing in this way.

Sometimes women tell me, "Oh, thank goodness, I thought I was losing my mind! I really thought I was losing my mind!" Yet it was just a physical thing. That's why you can have that verbal battle with your husband and ten minutes later he's standing there leering at you.

He's all ready for sex now, and you say, "You animal, how can you be like that?" But he says, "What's the matter?" The emotion of the argument is all over for him, but you're still all wrapped up in it.

A woman tends to react quickly in situations; a man tends to stand back and evaluate.

Sixty Rabbits

Women tend to become involved easily and quickly, but men tend to stand back and evaluate. She sees two darling little rabbits and says, "Oh, George, they're so cute and fuzzy, we need them." She sees only the two, but he sees a generation of about sixty! Because men stand back and evaluate situations, we often think, "Oh, he moves so slow!" We're always ready to jump in. All someone has to say is, "If you do this, that will happen," and we say, "Great! let's do it." But he says, "Hold it—let's wait." When you think he's being slow, remember that what he's really doing is evaluating. God made him like that for a good reason.

Women tend to react openly to situations and people while men tend to react inwardly and matter-of-factly. He's receiving information all the time, and that's why he just reacts matter-of-factly to things. We women have a tendency to react openly to situations even when we're quiet. A woman can usually read another woman even when she's not responding verbally, but men just go on their way.

Women tend to never forget; men tend to have to be reminded again and again.

Ah, Sweet Memories?

Men tend to have to be told again and again, but women tend to never forget. Now this can be bad, this tendency never to forget, because it can work against you if you don't keep it in control. You'll bring up bad memories during moments of stress, pulling something from the garbage pit from years back. So realize that you tend to do this. On the other hand, men need to be told again and again. They need gentle reminders about things. We had a leaky roof problem, and I had to gently remind Bill several times before we got anything done about it. (In the meantime, I was manning the bucket brigade!) He would open his "file drawer" of problems, drop the leaky roof problem in, close the file, and that would take care of it for him. So, use gentle reminders without nagging. I would just say to Bill, "Honey, your tabernacle's leaking." "Oh, yeah, yeah, I've got to do something about that." Remember, gentle reminders without nagging him, not "If you don't get that roof fixed I'll . . . ."

Sex All Day Long

Sex for a woman is what goes on all day long. I don't mean that this is necessarily what you're thinking about all day long, but that you need considerable preparation for the act itself. Sex for a man is what goes on in the bedroom. He comes home from work, has dinner, goes in the living room, and sits down. You see the backside of his newspaper for an hour, then maybe he does some work he brings home from the office, or maybe he works

To a woman sex is what goes on all day; to a man sex is what goes on in the bedroom.

on the car, or putters in the yard, or whatever, but in any case he hasn't talked to you all evening. Then it's time to go to bed, so you go in the bedroom, the door closes, and there he is with, "You little wench, you!" And you reply, "You haven't talked to me all night long, and now all of a sudden you want this. You animal! You're so insensitive and unfeeling!" That's the way he is, because for him sex is what goes on in the bedroom.

But sex for you is when he says things like, "Boy, that's a good dinner, Honey—you must have really worked hard on that. you smell good—what perfume is that? You always look so nice when I come home at night." You know what he's doing when he says those things? He's wooing you to the bedroom. And men need to know this. They need to know that women need to hear things that will woo them and prepare them for the bedroom, that they can't just walk in cold and expect their wives to be immediately "turned on" sexually. Women need to hear those little endearing words all evening long.

Every now and then I get a call, answer the phone, and hear a voice on the other end of the line say, "I love you." It usually comes about four o'clock in the afternoon, and fortunately it's always my husband! When he says, "I love you," I just melt. I decide right then that I'm going to start dinner. Even though I'd been planning on giving him some soup, now I'm going to give him something better! And when he comes home he compliments me on the dinner, always. And that's good. He asks me about my day, and that too is a part of preparing. He's learned, you see, how to prepare me. I love to hear those things, and I need to be wooed to the bedroom scene.

Hearing Versus Seeing

What is sexually stimulating to a woman is what she feels and hears. "I love you" just melts you. You love to hear those little endearments: "Gee, you look nice, you smell so good, I like the way you wear your hair." When he says those things and looks at you, you just melt. But what is sexually stimulating to a man is what he sees. Isn't that the truth! Now will you remember that? What is sexually stimulating to a man is what he *sees*.

Women are sexually stimulated by what they hear; men are sexually stimulated by what they see.

The Dirty White Robe

What does he see when he goes to work in the morning, as he leaves you at the front door? What do you look like? And what do you look like when he comes home? See to it that you're clean and that you're wearing something attractive. It only takes me two minutes. I know because I timed myself after I once made a big boo-boo. I was very careful what I looked like when he came home, but you should have seen what I looked like when he left in the morning! I had on these tired and dirty slippers and this stained terrycloth robe with holes where the ties came. It was the ugliest thing you ever saw. Then I thought to myself, "This is ridiculous. I'm forgetting something. How does he see all those women out there? They always look their best, and this is the way he sees me. This is the picture he carries of me all day long." It only takes me two minutes to wash my face, brush my teeth, and put on a nice robe, and then I say something like, "See you tonight." And he smiles. Remember that what your husband *sees* is what is stimulating to him sexually, so watch how you look around him.

What image of you does your husband carry with him all day?

Women tend to respond slowly sexually; men tend to respond quickly sexually.

It Takes Time

A woman tends to respond slowly sexually, while a man tends to respond quickly. You'd be surprised how few women refuse to accept this fact and say, "Something is wrong with me." It takes the average woman about thirty minutes to be aroused sexually, so realize that you are not some frigid thing—that it just takes you a little longer.

A woman needs to be loved, but a man needs to be admired. And there's always something that you can admire about your man. This one gal had a husband who was just like a beanpole, thin as a rail, so she went home

Women need to be loved; men need to be admired.

after one of these seminars, sat down beside him on the couch, put her hand up on his muscle and said "Ummm." Do you know, he started lifting weights! He was out there every day because she admired his teensy tiny muscles. Now he thinks she's terrific because she's so smart to recognize how wonderful he is.

A woman needs to hear words in order to know that she's receiving understanding. You need to hear him say, "I understand. I know how it is. I know, Honey, I know it hurts, I know, I know. I understand." The man needs a good listener to know he's receiving understanding. He needs to look at the expression on her face as he's just pouring it out, telling her how he handled this big deal and so forth. And she need to think he's terrific, just terrific. One time Bill had a real nitty-gritty problem in his job that he was sharing with me, and just like that I saw the answer, so I said, "Bill, why don't you do this and do that, and see how it works out?" But he looked at me and said, "I'll solve it." In other words, he didn't want me to solve it for him—he just wanted me to listen. He didn't ask for my opinion—he just asked for my ears. I learned quickly on that one! What men want is our whole attention—not wandering around while we're talking, but eye-to-eye contact and real listening.

A woman needs feedback to know she's receiving understanding; a man needs a good listener.

A man tends to be stubborn; a woman tends to be traditional.

Ham in the Pan

Men tend to be stubborn—"I won't change, it's not my fault"—while women tend to be traditional—"I've always done it this way and there's no reason to change." Now see how you can come to an impasse here. "I've always done it this way. My mother did it this way and my grandmother did it this way, so there's no reason to change. It was good enough for them and it's good enough for me." In the meantime he's saying, "I will not change, it's not my fault," so you get into this problem together.

A husband asked his wife why she always cut the ends off the ham, and she replied that her mother always did it that way. When his mother-in-law came to visit he asked *her* why she did that, and she replied "That's the way *my* mother always did it." Finally he asked the grandma, and she replied, "That's the only way it would fit into the pan!" Often we hold to traditions which have now become ridiculous.

Men tend to demand proof before moving, while women tend to move on promises alone. I tell you, give a woman a promise and off she goes. That's why you move so quickly in the spiritual. Jesus gives you a promise and off you go. His promise is good enough for you. The man says, "Now, wait a minute; let's look at this carefully. What does Paul say? What does Peter say? Did it work in the Book of Acts? Well, okay." That's why he's solid, why when he gets the truth he hangs onto it and moves on it. Ten weeks later you think about that same promise that sent you off like gangbusters and you say, "Oh, I don't know if it works or

A man needs proof before proceeding; a woman moves on a promise alone.

not." But he gets it and hangs on to it. You make a beautiful balance this way because he gets all the documents and proof and then moves. He's absolutely convinced it's going to work, and he'll rarely move off his conviction.

Women tend to be idealistic and romantic; men tend to be practical, down-to-earth.

Kissing on the Beach

Women tend to be romantic and idealistic while men tend to be practical and objective. He calls you one night and says, "Let's go out to dinner tonight," and you say, "Terrific!" Now what you're thinking is, "Let's see, I think maybe we'll go to the Islandia on Mission Bay and then we'll go down to the beach and walk along the water. We'll hold hands in the moonlight. We'll embrace and he'll kiss me." But he's thinking, "Now let's see, we'll grab a quick bite somewhere, and if we hurry we'll catch the Padre ball game, and if we leave real quick we can dash home and catch the end of the Dodger game on TV." Believe me, you're going to have a problem that evening!

Women tend to play games, but men tend to be direct. Your husband will come up to you and say, "Honey, what's the matter?" You respond, "Nothing. Nothing." He says, "Honey, something's wrong. I can tell something's wrong." "No." "Oh, come on, Honey, level with me, I know something's really bothering you. What did I do?" "Nothing." And all the time you're playing games with him. Finally he says "Well, okay,"

Women tend to "play games" with their husbands.

and you burst into tears. Confused, he says, "What's wrong?" and you reply, "You never understand." You see, you don't want to have to tell him what's wrong, because if you tell him and he does what he was supposed to do if you *didn't* tell him, it won't be as good as if you didn't tell him and he did it anyway! In other words, you want him to do something without having to tell him. So you play these games, and the poor man's so confused he doesn't know which end's up. And to top it all off, you end up being mad at him for three days, and the problem never gets resolved. Tell him what the trouble is so he can rectify it, and then he'll be built up because he's handled it right, and you'll think he's wonderful. Don't play games with him. Get it straightened out.

Appreciate Your Man

A man needs to be accepted, admired, respected, adapted to, and appreciated. Let me say something about appreciation. Most women don't really know what it is to carry the responsibility of supporting a family financially. Women who have had to face this position, either through divorce or widowhood, have discovered the tremendous weight that goes along with raising a family with all its material needs. We have no idea what that weight is if we haven't actually supported a family financially. So appreciate what he does as the breadwinner. Don't make light of it. If he can appreciate the meals you set before him, and how you handle his money, then *you* appreciate how *he* arrives at that money and what he goes through to bring it home.

Also, a man needs to be *desired*. Now, this, to a man, is being loved. When these things are happening in his life, he knows that he is loved. "However, let each man of you (without exception) love his wife as [being in a sense] his very own self; and let the wife see that she respects and reverences her husband—that she notices him, regards him, honors him, prefers him, venerates and esteems him; and that she defers to him, praises him, and loves and admires him exceedingly" (Ephesians 5:33 *The Amplified New Testament*).* First Peter 3:2 says, "When they observe the pure and modest way in which you conduct yourselves, together with your reverence [for your husband. That is, you are to feel for him all that reverence includes]—to respect, defer to, revere him; [revere means] to honor, esteem (appreciate, prize), and [in the human sense] adore him; [and adore means] to admire, praise, be devoted to deeply love and enjoy [your husband]."*

Cherished and Encouraged

A woman needs to be *cherished* and constantly *encouraged*. We need to be *cared for*, and that means both materially and spiritually. But I'll tell you one thing—if a woman know she's loved, she can live in meager surroundings without complaint. Some men make the mistake of just giving women things, things, and more things, without loving them and caring for them.

A woman also needs to be *sought out*. It's a wise husband who seeks out his wife's counsel and opinion.

---

* *The Amplified New Testament*, copyright ©1958 by The Lockman Foundation. Used by permission.

Abraham was told by God, "Listen to Sarah." When you got married you didn't put your mind in neutral. Your mind is to be used by God in the problems that you have together and in solving them. Some of you are very bright women, and you can bring a great deal to your husband's ministry and work by helping him in this way.

A woman also needs to be appreciated. Let me share with you one occasion when Bill showed such appreciation of me. It was a particularly harrowing Monday for me. It had been terribly busy, with people going and coming like Grand Central Station all day long, and now on the spur of the moment we found ourselves with two extra guests for dinner. In the hustle of trying to keep things in some semblance of order, I had neglected the cooking time of the meatloaf and it had burned badly. It was all I had to serve, so I put it on the table with profuse apologies and much embarrassment because it was the first time these two people had been to dinner in our home, and I wasn't all that thrilled that it had to be meatloaf in the first place! Our male guest looked at the meatloaf and said, "We can see it's burned; it really does look bad, and apologies won't help the looks of it." I saw Bill's eye flash, and then as I was serving the meatloaf he looked at me with great love and said in a voice that everyone heard, "I'll have a large piece of meatloaf, please, Honey." I appreciated so much his consideration of what I was going through in those moments!

Now see the difference between these lists. The only thing that's the same is "appreciated." We both need to be appreciated by our mates, yet the needs a man has in order to know he is loved are completely different from those of a woman.

Leader and Leaner

I want to share a small teaching from Ken Poure. If you've never seen Ken perform a marriage, go if you have the opportunity. It's the most beautiful thing you'll ever see. It is the only wedding I have ever attended when, after the bride and groom were presented to the congregation, we all stood up and applauded. Isn't that something? It was glorious—we all sang "To God be the glory, great things He hath done." It was beautiful. You may think that sounds a little raucous, but it wasn't.

Just before the wedding vows Ken gave a little sermonette. He said something like this: "*The man is a leader*, and this is the way God planned it. *The woman is a leaner*, for God has made us to be leaners and responders." This doesn't mean that your brain is in neutral. It just means that you need to lean. You can lean and think at the same time. Don't mistakenly feel that this makes you less intelligent. All these differences listed between men and women have nothing to do with intellect. It doesn't mean that one partner is smarter than the other. It just means that there's a difference in female responses because God planned it this way.

The man is to be a learner and so is *the wife to be a learner*. This is the process that you go through for all the years of your marriage. You're constantly learning. *He is to be a lover* and *you are to be a lover*. Learn to be married lovers. Has that ever occurred to you? Learn to set the scene for married lovers. Do you ever pull out the stops, setting candles on the table, dressing pretty, fixing a good meal, and shoving the kids off on a neighbor with the promise, "I'll do the same for you tomorrow night?"

Sure, some of us did this during college days—shifting the kids around so we could have times alone with our husband's—but how about now? Learn to be married lovers. Your husband will love you for it! He'll feel so content with you that other women won't mean much to him; you'll be satisfying all his desires. I'm so glad God knows what He's doing! It's a good feeling to know that He understands us all, that He knows right where we are, and His ways are perfect!

 CHAPTER 6

Techniques
in the Bedroom

Now we're going to talk about techniques, and this is where everybody says, "Lock the doors, don't let anybody in or out!" But it's really not that bad. I'll be teaching general truths, and God will take care of the methods and ways for individual couples. There's a difference between being indiscreet and being honest. I could say many true things, but some of them might not be *discreet* to say in a book like this. I'll present some general truths, and then with the guidance of the Holy Spirit you'll come into the full truth for yourself and with your mate. But I won't cop out or beat around the bush, as you'll see.

What we want to aim for is abandon and freedom in the marriage bed with your husband. God wants you to be able, without guilt, or little foxes, or shadows of forebodings, to come to your marriage bed with absolute abandon, ready to love your husband and to be loved and to demonstrate that together. God leaves some things unsaid because they vary with each individual couple. What is right for one couple is not necessarily right for every other couple. That doesn't mean it's wrong, but only that it's not right for that couple. Do we understand each other? "It is right to be concerned about the mutual sexual adjustment in *your* marriage and to give constant attention to learning the skills that will enrich your sex relationship!"* It's not something you learn overnight, or in the reading of one book; only during years of being together will you learn these skills of lovemaking with your husband. And you *should* give attention to them. There is much bondage in this area because of what Satan has done. If he can separate the man and woman here, he's got a good thing going, so determine not to let that happen.

Move Toward Harmony

I'd like to give you a quote from *Letters to Philip* by Charlie Shedd (Pages 110, 111): "Freedom to express your desires is a great goal, but for the first twenty years remember it's more goal than reality. Sure an uninhibited sex life is what you want. But you won't get it by crushing her ideas of how it should be with your ideas of how it should be." (This is written to his son, by the way.) "The eventual aim is total freedom to experiment and let yourself go. There are infinite variations in a full sex life and numberless approaches. The fact is that *nothing you do in marriage is wrong provided it doesn't hurt*

---

* Petersen and Smith, *Two Become One* (Family Concern, 1973) p. 63. Used by permission.

either member to the union emotionally or physically. But that last word is loaded. Unless you bring her along slowly you may destroy more in one night than it would take years to recover. So the wise husband paces himself with infinite tenderness! He moves toward harmony slowly."*

Then I have another quote for you from *Sexual Happiness in Marriage*, by Herbert Miles (pages 77, 78): "In interpersonal relationships in the community and society, modesty is a queen among virtues, but in the privacy of the marriage bedroom, behind locked doors, and in the presence of pure married love, there is no such thing as modesty." Please remember that it says in Genesis that they were both naked and were not ashamed. (I know of one couple who have been married several years, yet she still continues to dress and undress in the bathroom!) In pure married love there is no such thing as modesty. "A couple should feel free to do whatever they both enjoy which moves them into a full expression of their mutual love in a sexual experience. At this point it is well to give a word of caution. *All sex experiences should be those which both husband and wife want. Neither, at any time, should force the other to do anything that he does not want to do. Love does not force.*" †

---

* From *Letters to Philip* by Charlie W. Shedd. Copyright © 1968 by Charlie W. Shedd and the Abundance Foundation. Published by Doubleday and Company, Inc. Used by permission.

† From *Sexual Happiness in Marriage*, by Herbert J. Miles. Copyright © 1967 by Zondervan Publishing House. Used by permission.

Tales and Trouble

I'd like to give you a couple more points. First let me caution you not to share the things that go on in your bedroom, the privacy of those acts together, with someone else, and by that I mean sharing those experiences verbally with another person. Don't tell tales *outside* the bedroom of what goes on *inside* the bedroom. I know of a daughter who shared with her mother some things in regard to her sex relationship with her husband, and a tremendous breach came between husband, wife, and mother, and that breach is there to this day. The mother was horrified at what went on in her daughter's bedroom, but the daughter had no business sharing that with her mother.

Another little gal came to me tremendously upset and in tears. She had shared with a close friend some of what went on in their lovemaking sessions together, and this friend said, "You don't do that, do you?" And my little friend was crushed. She was floating between right and wrong and God's will and what her husband desired. She was really messed up. Don't share with others. The one exception is a competent, godly counselor you know you can trust. Then you know that what you say will stay with him or her and will not go outside that counseling room. We have no business judging the lovemaking that goes on in other people's bedrooms. So be very careful with whom you share and what you share.

God's Abandon

I would like to add some other cautions. When we

talk about the sexual freedom that Miles talks about here, he is of course *not* talking about such things as wife-swapping or these clubs that say, "Let us enrich your marriage together." He's *not* talking about that. Now you might think it's silly that I even have to mention this, but believe me it's not. God calls wife-swapping adultery. Also, Miles is not referring to anything masochistic or sadistic. That is not glorifying to God. Anyone who needs to inflict or receive pain to reach his or her sexual peak is psychologically disturbed. God did not intend for it to be this way, and I strongly urge those people to seek counsel quickly.

The Abandon of Love

Love always seeks whatever is the highest good for both the individuals and the two together. Remember, we're endeavoring to bring you into an abandon. When I say "abandon" a cold chill sometimes goes over people. But I mean abandon in the marriage bed with your husband. You are God's gift to him, and you are his helper. You are intended by God to enjoy one another physically, and at the same time you have that added benefit of "nourishing the one." What could be better? It's so beautiful, yet we think there's got to be something wrong with it somewhere. So we hunt, hunt, hunt, trying to find what's wrong, and usually we come up with some guilt in some area. What I'm trying to do is to bring you into that freedom with your husband in the marriage bed which God intended for you, so that you might truly enjoy one another and be satisfied and fulfilled. Satan has robbed women of this satisfaction, but there's no need to stay unsatisfied.

Remember that sex is communication on all three levels: body, soul, and spirit. If what you're doing sexually doesn't communicate love, gratification, and heightened enjoyment, you're missing what God intended for you. If your sex experience doesn't communicate to him and he to you love, gratification, and heightened enjoyment, you're missing something important. If you come away from the bed feeling dejected, depressed, and guilt-ridden, something is terribly wrong, so see what it is, look at it, and move into the freedom God wants for you. Oh, will your husband be happy! And when he's happy, you'll be even happier, and you'll be like newlyweds.

I wish I could show you some women I know who have been married 25 and 30 years. Wow, what they've got going! You'd be surprised. I used to think it was all over when you reach forty, and oh, those poor people at fifty! You know that old phrase, "Life begins at forty." And it's true. You young ones think you have it made, but let me tell you, you haven't seen anything yet! You've got terrific things ahead of you, so be ready to receive them. You think you have it good now. You just wait. If you've got a good thing going, it can get better. So come into freedom.

Fear in Sex

I want to share with you about fear in sex. Someone will say to me, "Everytime my husband touches me, or when I know he wants to go to bed with me, a cold chill comes over me and everything in me just stops because I know what he's going to want to do." And she'll name something that her whole body rebels against. If you find that this is where you are at some point in your sex relationship with your husband, that everything in you crashes to a halt, I want to give you this little hint. I want you to talk to him and say (not in these words, please— you choose your own words), "I want to give myself to you in real freedom." Let him know that. "I want to give myself to you in real freedom and abandon," and get that settled. Then say, "I'm going to do that. I'm going to trust you to bring me along to your satisfaction and to mine, and I'm going to love you and recognize that you are my other half." And when you're communicating this to him you're going to tell him what it is that distresses you. You know what he's going to do? He will hear you and see your need, and a protectiveness will generate within him for you.

I sent a young gal home to tell her husband just that. She shared with him what distressed her, but then she said, "I want to surrender to you, I really do, Honey, I really do, and I love you, and I'm going to trust you." My goodness, he just put his arms around her and said, "You haven't got anything to worry about, Honey, nothing." His response was a sweet protectiveness. She came up to me several weeks later and said, "Do you remember, I talked to you about this?" And I did remember. She's so darling, I couldn't forget her—so babelike, so childlike, and she received my counsel so sweetly. And I said, "Well, how is it going?" And she said, "You just wouldn't believe it, he did just what you said he'd do." "Oh, thank you, God." "And he just protected me and he understood. Mary, he *understood!*" In her exuberance she started to tell me what they had done to resolve the problem, but I stopped her. I said, "That's between the two of you." I don't know how you resolved it. I just know that you did, and that's what's glorifying to God, the fact that you met it together." If you have fear in this area, something that your husband desires that you don't enjoy, just tell him. You cannot expect him to understand something that bothers you until you have told him what it is!

Do Your Own Thing

Don't be threatened about what other people say about their sexual behavior, their do's and don't's. If someone says, "Don't you ever do that, it's awful, a Christian doesn't do that," don't listen and don't be threatened. Just close your ears to it and say thank you very much, and then go your way. Don't be threatened by other people's do's and don't's. Also, don't be threatened by national averages. Do you know that the national average says that the average couple has sex relations 3.4 times a week? I've often wondered about that .4! Right there some of you are having a problem, because some of you are thinking, "I knew he was oversexed," and others are saying, "My gosh, we're behind, maybe something's wrong with him." Some husbands actually keep count, you know—"You still owe me one." Don't be threatened by such national averages, but instead concentrate on meeting one another's needs. Now that's a big difference. You will probably find that your amount is more or less than the national average, but just concentrate on meeting one another's needs, and you'll be fine.

Sex is not a sideline in marriage. It is a major gift given in a major, divine vocation. Don't ever forget that. It's not something you can let sit on the shelf and use every now and then. You know, "Okay, let's get it over with; satisfy yourself, animal." Oh no. God did not make sex only for the man. He meant it as the gift that would unite two people into one. God saw everything, and behold, it was very good. That includes sex!

Solomon's Song of Love

Now let's turn to the Song of Solomon. This is the one book of the Bible you always hope your children will never discover. "Oh, God, don't let them find that one, they're too young!" A friend of mine stopped in for tea a few days ago and during the conversation laughingly told me that her teenage daughter had just finished reading Song of Solomon and with eyes saucer-big had informed her mother that she had never, ever seen Scripture like that before. Now I know there's a marvelous spiritual teaching in this book which describes how Christ relates to the believer. It's a beautiful teaching. If you've never gone through a study of the Song of Solomon with that teaching of Christ relating to the believer, you've missed a blessing. It's just beautiful. However, right now we're talking about the flesh-and-blood people in the Song of Solomon. We're talking about Solomon and his bride, because this is a story about married lovers. We're going to see how they respond to one another.

The first technique I want to talk about is *abandon*. An example of this is in Song of Solomon 6:3, and it's a beautiful song that you all sing: "I am my beloved's and my beloved is mine." Praise the Lord, abandon and possessiveness! There is absolutely nothing wrong with being taken for granted. I love it. I love knowing that Bill loves me and possesses me, that I am his and that there's a certain "for granted" in there that's good. I like knowing that he knows I'm his, exclusively so. I am my beloved's and he is mine. It works both ways. No double standard here. He's all mine and I'm all his, and I wouldn't have it any other way. God has given you the freedom and privilege of expressing this abandon physically with your husband in the marriage bed. Aren't you glad?

Abandon in Speech

The second point is *abandon in speech*. In Song of Solomon chapter 7 we see a dialogue between lovers. Starting with verse 6 he says to her, "How beautiful and how delightful you are, my love, with all your charms! Your stature is like a palm tree, and your breasts are like its clusters. I said, 'I will climb the palm tree, I will take hold of its fruit stalks.' Oh, may your breasts be like clusters of the vine and the fragrance of your breath like apples, and your mouth like the best wine! It goes down smoothly for my beloved, flowing gently through the lips of those who fall asleep" (verses 6-9). Oh, my goodness! That's in the Bible! Good grief! Who'd have ever thought it! Isn't that beautiful—he speaks to her and says things aloud to her.

Let's look next at chapter 2, verse 14. Here he says, "O my dove, in the clefts of the rock, in the secret place of the steep pathway, let me see your form, let me hear your voice, for your voice is sweet and your form is lovely." Doesn't that do something to you? I tell you, sometimes when I'm struggling into my pantyhose or something, and I look at myself in the mirror, I think, "Ugh." Bill can walk by and say "Ah!" and the whole image changes—suddenly I'm Sophia Loren. Words, little inflections like that, can mean so much. Abandon in speech! Trust between a man and wife is built by communication, by saying these things to one another.

Now back to Song of Solomon. In chapter 7, verses 10-13, she says, "I am my beloved's and his desire is for me. Come, my beloved, let us go out into the country, let us spend the night in the villages. Let us rise early and go to the vineyards; let us see whether the vine has budded and its blossoms have opened, and whether the pomegranates have bloomed. There I will give you my love. The mandrakes have given forth fragrance, and over our doors are all choice fruits, both new and old, which I have saved up for you, my beloved." Oh, my goodness, that is absolutely beautiful! I can see you tonight in the closet with a flashlight going over the Song of Solomon to be inspired. But this is beautiful, this abandon in speech. Now I know you won't say it exactly like that. If he began saying to you, "Your breasts are like clusters and I will climb the palm tree and take hold of its fruits" you'd say, "Hold it! Wait a minute! What's the matter with you?"

One gal who has heard this teaching numerous times always gets the giggles at this point. And for a while I could never really understand what she found so hysterical in these beautiful portions of Scripture. One day as we were having lunch with a group of women, discussing this particular section, she started again. Between tears of laughter she managed to choke out, "I think this woman is something else. You should see the picture I have of her in my mind's eye. If my husband told me I had breasts like clusters of dates, I wouldn't be pleased. In fact, the bedroom would be number 1000 on my list of priorities for that day."

But he says other things you like, and you know you like them and need to hear them. You need to hear him say those things to you, those little flirty things just between the two of you, things that inspire and excite you. And you should say them to him. Remember, he's receiving information and he'll put it in his little file and remember it.

Communicating in the Bedroom

Now let me give you two Scriptures about communicating. In Song of Solomon 1:13, she says, "My beloved is to me a pouch of myrrh which lies all night between my breasts. My beloved is to me a cluster of henna blossoms." And then he responds to her with, "How beautiful you are, my darling, how beautiful you are! Your eyes are like doves." She responds by saying, "How handsome you are, my beloved, and so pleasant! Indeed, our couch is luxuriant!" Boy! Now that's good! "Indeed our couch is luxuriant." Speech, abandon in speech. Say it aloud to him. Let him hear of your love.

A verse in the New Testament, Colossians 4:6, says, "Let your speech always be with grace, seasoned as it were with salt." We think of that everywhere except in the marriage bed. "Let your speech always be with grace." Ephesians 4:29 says, "Let no unwholesome word proceed from your mouth, but only such a word as is good for edification according to the need of the moment, that it may give grace to those who hear." Isn't that good? Grace is divine influence, and so your speech should be according to the need of the moment, so that it might give divine influence. And it's also needed in the marriage bed. Speech, so that he can hear and know what it is that you like, what you think of him, and how it feels to be with him, all snuggled up and safe and secure and loved by him. He will receive information and it will build him and edify him. An *unwholesome word* is any word that tears down, and we women are masters at that. We can tear down in one word. We need to learn to speak words of grace that edify the heart that hears.

Appreciating the Body

The next point is that we need a *healthy appreciation of the human body*. Song of Solomon chapter 4, verses 1-7, says, "How beautiful you are, my darling, how beautiful you are! Your eyes are like doves behind your veil; your hair is like a flock of goats that have descended from Mount Gilead. Your teeth are like a flock of newly shorn ewes which have come up from their washing, all of which bear twins, and not one among them has lost her young. Your lips are like a scarlet thread, and your mouth is lovely. Your temples are like a slice of a pomegranate behind your veil. Your neck is like the tower of David built with rows of stones, on which are hung a thousand shields, all the round shields of the mighty men. Your two breasts are like two fawns, twins of a gazelle, which feed among the lilies. Until the cool of the day when the shadows flee away, I will go my way to the mountain of myrrh and to the hill of frankincense. You are altogether beautiful, my darling, and there is no blemish in you."

Bill makes me feel absolutely beautiful. At first that seems silly, because when you look at me you say, "Hey, you're not so great!" But he makes me feel beautiful, just beautiful. And he's the one I want to please. When he thinks I'm beautiful and tells me that, I feel wonderful, and there isn't anything I wouldn't do for him. He's so smart!

Now listen to this. She says in Song of Solomon chapter 5, verses 10-16, "My beloved is dazzling and ruddy, outstanding among ten thousand. His hand is like gold, pure gold; his locks are like clusters of dates, and black as a raven. His eyes are like doves beside streams of water, bathed in milk and reposed in their setting. His cheeks are like a bed of balsam, banks of sweet-scented herbs; his lips are lilies, dripping with liquid myrrh. His hands are rods of gold set with beryl; his abdomen is carved ivory inlaid with sapphires. His legs are pillars of alabaster set on pedestals of pure gold; his appearance is like Lebanon, choice as the cedars. His mouth is full of sweetness, and he is wholly desirable. This is my beloved and this is my friend, O daughters of Jerusalem." I tell you, I don't see how any woman can read these Scriptures and not be inspired to go home and throw her arms around her husband, even if he's 4 foot 6 or 6 foot 4, and say, "You're beautiful and I love you."

"This is my beloved and this is my friend." There's your Scripture for friendship. The highest fulfillment of friendship is marriage. "My beloved and my friend." I don't care what he looks like. I don't care if he's Mr. Adonis or Mr. Peepers, a muscle man or a little guy and not good-looking at all. You tell him he's wonderful and he'll think you're very smart to recognize that. Some of us are so stingy with our compliments and words of encouragement, fearing we will somehow be depleted if we speak them. If you've never complimented your man, if you've never built him up and spoken to him words that he enjoys hearing, you have no idea what you have coming to you. There isn't anything he won't do for you if he knows he's loved like that.

Clean and Attractive

The closeness of physical intimacy in marriage really requires us to be clean and attractive. Proverbs 31:30 tells us that being a personal peacock is vain and deceptive, but to think appearance is of no consequence at all is just downright foolish. Don't think that because you're already married that's the end of your obligation to stay attractive. No, keep yourself attractive. Now some of you have no trouble spending money on yourself. You're buying new clothes for yourself all the time. So you can just skip the next paragraph.

This paragraph is for those of you who are like me, who go around with your panties at half-mast because you've got them pinned, since they've long ago separated from the elastic at the waist. This is for you who have your bras pinned with some little thing and underwear that should have been in the rag bag months ago. Go buy yourself some nice underwear. Your husband is the only person beside yourself who sees it, but buy it anyway. Purchase a georgeous nightgown. Don't go to bed every night in some Grandma Moses thing that looks like you expect to bed down in an igloo, or some old rag that's so threadbare it looks like decay has already set in. Don't look dowdy. Look cute, or attractive, or voluptuous, or whatever your personality calls for you to look like when you go to bed. *None* of you have the personality of looking crummy when you go to bed. Some of you can look very sexy-cute while others of you are the slinky type, but just be sure to look nice. Then get yourself a nice robe in which to kiss him good-bye in the morning.

A few years ago I was shopping for the first of our yearly honeymoons, and I was buying a regular trousseau for myself just like a new bride. I had already bought myself two new nightgowns when I walked by this one rack and saw this gorgeous black lace thing. I looked at it and said, "oh, that is gorgeous!" But then I said, "no, forget it. I already have two nighties, so this one would be absolutely frivolous. No, I won't buy it." My friend who was with me said, "Mary, I don't want you to think of this as an expenditure; think of it as an investment." So I went over and took the nightie off the rack and told the salesgirl, "Wrap it up!" I want you to think of it this way, not as an expenditure but as an investment. Your husband will appreciate the fact that you care what you look like when you go to bed at night. When you put your underwear on and he's the only one who ever sees it, he'll appreciate the fact that you care how you look for him.

If he likes you to wear perfume, do it. Do what he likes. Don't let somebody else tell you what to do. Do what *he* likes. Maybe someone won't approve of what you do, but you be obedient to *him*. There isn't a man alive who doesn't feel proud to walk down the street with an attractive woman on his arm. Make sure you're that woman!

Giving Before Feeling

Love is physically expressed, so it should be exhilarating and it should be anticipated. Love is not only a feeling, but it's an act of *giving* long before it's a feeling. This is love in action. Song of Solomon chapter 1, verse 2, says, "May he kiss me with the kisses of his mouth! For your love is better than wine." Anticipate love, so that you can hardly wait to kiss him hello and tell him how much you love him. Does he love to come home? He should. I think I can honestly say that Bill does. Coming home is the best part of his day, even when he's tired and not feeling good. And it's the highlight of *my* day, too.

Learn to evoke the desired responses from your partner. This is especially for those of you who have unresponsive mates. Wonder of wonders, some of you are married to husbands who are not responsive to you! I want to give you some help, and I'm going to give you several suggestions. First, it is not unfeminine to be the aggressor in the relationship, and don't let anyone tell you it is. Nothing is more feminine. You flirted with him before you got married, didn't you?

Don't Give Up

Don't give up—it takes time. Most women don't know what it's like to be rejected in the marriage bed because *they* are the ones who do the rejecting! But I have also counseled with women who have been refused in the marriage bed over and over and over again. I know it hurts right to the core of you when your husband does that. It is not pleasant. It has been clinically proven that continued rejection is the hardest blow to the mental, emotional, and physical systems. Those who have experienced this would concur with me. Rejection often takes the path of neglect, a pathway which kills relationships and sometimes even kills people.

It is essential that you try to get over the fear of rejection. Now I understand that this is hard. Trying to evoke the desired responses in your partner and receiving one rejection after another takes a lot of prayer on your part. If you have this problem, find someone you trust to pray with you about it. And again I say, don't give up. It takes time.

Learn to Forgive

Learn to forgive your husband for rejecting you. Don't carry the resentment and bitterness. Somehow get out of your rut. Buy a new nightgown, fix up the bedroom, do your hair differently, buy a candle, buy a plant—do *something* that will bring a little inspiration to you as well as to him.

Becoming Aware

Become aware of your husband's needs. Don't

assume that you know them all. You know a few of his needs, but not all of them. So take a deep breath, sit down with him, and say, "Honey, what would you like? Where am I not fulfilling in the marriage bed? And then hang on, because he'll tell you. Don't ask him in the attitude that there's no way you could be failing to meet his needs. That's what I thought: "Oh, tell me, Honey," all the while thinking there wouldn't be any unmet needs. "How would you like it, in a list of threes or fours?" And he told me. So don't assume you know, because he's tucked a lot of things away in his heart. Ask him. Say, "I want to know because I want to fulfill those needs. I know as I do that I'm going to benefit too, and we're going to be nourished together." So ask him and become aware of his needs, but don't ask him unless you intend to meet them.

Tell Him What You Like

Let your husband know what you like. One young girl who had been married just a few months came up to me after one of my seminars and said there was something she liked very much, but her husband wasn't doing it. I said, "Why are you telling me?" "Well, you said any of us who had a problem could come up." So I said, "Go home and tell *him*." "*Tell* him?" "Well, of course, he's the one who needs to know. *Share* with him what you like." When she went home it took her about sixty seconds to tell him and he said, "Oh? okay!" Later she phoned me and reported, "I did it. I told him, and now everything's just great."

So many wives live in misery and unfulfillment just

because they won't talk with their husbands. What better person to tell than him? He's your marriage partner. He's your lover. Tell him what you like, so he can satisfy you and bring you into fulfillment. Then he'll feel good too. You know, when we please each other and bring pleasure to one another, that builds us up. Remember what we said happens and should happen in the marriage relationship. He will also be built up because he will be bringing satisfaction to you. So share with him these things that you desire. Don't keep them all tucked away.

Keep the bedroom clean and uncluttered.

Keep Your Bedroom Clean

Here's something obvious, yet neglected: keep your bedroom clean. Oh, dear ones, you would be surprised what that master bedroom is used for. You have laundry waiting to be folded. You have laundry waiting to be ironed. You have a pile of laundry waiting to be mended. You have various toys, broken and otherwise, sitting there for who-knows-what, you have papers around, tape recorders, etc. If you can find the bed, you feel you've accomplished quite a bit. Keep that bedroom nice. That's the first room I do every day. I have a lot of plants in our bedroom, and the whole scene is blues and greens. It's a luscious room, always neat and clean and always smelling good. It's bright and airy and wonderful. Now when your bedroom's a mess, he might not think that's affecting him, but it really is. And it's affecting you too. Who wants to go into that ugly room and feel romantic if there's all that stuff around? All you can think of is "Oh, I've got laundry and I've got to put those away and look at that ironing" and on and on and on. Stuff it in a closet, do anything, but get it out of the bedroom.

Save Your Energy

Be sure to save your prime energy for your husband. Get your priorities right. If it's going to knock you under the table to scrub the kitchen floor, don't scrub it—let it wait until tomorrow. Now some of you may just need to get yourselves organized. If you have to get a "running start" to get all the way across your kitchen floor to keep from sticking to spilled gravy, dribbled Pepsi, and crushed Oreos, you know that floor should have been scrubbed long ago.

Get your work schedule put together in a way that doesn't leave you with tons of work on any one particular day. Keep things in order, so you can save your time and energy for him, so that every night when you crawl into bed you won't say, "Oh, I'm so tired," and all he's thought about all day is getting home. He's waited through dinner and he's waited through the kids going to bed, and now when he gets you in there you say, "Oh, I'm so tired." And he says, "Oh, crumb!" Last night it was a headache, the night before that something else.

How do you look when you retire at night?

Save your prime energy for him. Now I know that with little kids it's hard. Sometimes the day goes from bad to rotten before the clock strikes 10 A.M. and by 5 P.M. you want to crawl into the baby's playpen and pull his blanket over your head. I've been there. But try to do the best you can. And be honest. Many times we use fatigue as an excuse.

Try to squeeze in some time to pretty up before he comes in the door at night.

A Little Help—Please!

I'd like to mention right here that working wives will need to have some "house help" from their husbands. Now maybe you're married to a "Felix" who has everything done before you've opened both eyes in the morning. But just in case you're not, I want to note that if the husband expects his wife to carry a part-time or full-time job, care for the children, be a gourmet cook, entertain guests frequently, and still be the loving, supportive wife he desires, he will need to either offer a helping hand or make some arrangements for help to come in.

If he refuses, while still insisting that all of the above continue to be carried out, he will in all probability have to either cart her off in a pine box or send her to the "funny farm"!

Working wives, part-time or full-time, need to have their husbands' physical help and kind support.

CHAPTER 7

The Touch of Love

Not long ago a nationally prominent doctor made a great discovery. This pediatrician, who treats critically ill babies and children, began letting the parents of these little ones come into that forbidden nursery in the hospital. He encouraged them to put their hands into the incubator and caress their child and lift him and hold him. He encouraged them to go into their child's sickroom and sit with him, staying with him all night if necessary. Anytime the baby cried, the parents were to hold him and caress him and rock him. And the doctor made this great discovery: the mortality rate began to drop. It had previously been quite high in this area of medicine because these critically ill babies and children had either heart, breathing, or intestinal troubles. Because of the touching that he was allowing the parents to do in these rooms which had previously been closed to them, the babies began rallying. He told the parents, "Please come and stay with your child; we'll put in a bed for you. If he cries, pick him up and rock him." As the parents did this the mortality rate went down and down and down. The importance of touch!

Jesus knew the importance of touch, and we need to know it too. We need to know how important it is to touch people. Now there's a whole teaching of touch in the world around us today, and I know there is the unholy, unclean touch, but I want to ignore that for now. It is because of this error that we are so afraid to touch one another as Jesus reached out and touched people. He longs to take your family unit and have touch going all through it. This is what I want you to see—that it's needed most in your family. There's the holy, pure touch we give to our brothers and sisters in Christ. This is the good and holy and pure touch of love that we should be extending to one another. This is that touch of compassion and caring and healing that Jesus gave all the time and still gives through us to one another. Many times when we pray with people nothing happens until the moment we touch them—then everthing breaks through. I don't understand it, I just know it works. The importance of touch is so vital as we work with people.

Be a Touching Person

Give one another opportunity for touch. In your family use that playful fun touch. If you say, "I'm just not a touching person, that's just not my personality," that's a cop-out. You cannot convince me you are not. Everyone has that capacity to touch, because God has the power to use us imperfect vessels as channels for His touch of love. And He most definitely desires touch among your family members. If you haven't been doing it, start. If you have a big strapping eighteen-year-old boy, I don't recommend that you go home and say, "Oh, Darling, I love you," and throw your arms around him. He'll probably throw up. He'll never accept that. And if you haven't been touching him all these years he'll think, "Mom has gone bananas, she's out of her tree. Watch out, Dad, you've got to commit her." But you can begin giving him opportunities for touch. "Hi, guy! Gee, you look sharp"—touch. Touch and go, those quick little touches. You see your husband sitting reading the paper —walk by and say, "Hi, Honey," pat pat, and go. No big deal, but you just communicated something to him— you said, "I see you, I love you, I care."

Do it with your kids. If you have little ones, you've got it made, so begin now. We were at dinner one night with this family when their big lug of a fifteen-year-old came out in his pajamas and said, "Night, Dad," went over to his mom and said, "Night, Mom" (smack) and lumbered off to bed. Terrific! They have a love relationship going that's healthy. You see, girls need Dad's touch and boys need Mom's touch. It's important in order to keep a good, healthy thing going in them toward the opposite sex. When your little gals get to be about five they're going to marry Daddy, remember? "How come I can't marry Daddy?" And then you have a son about that age who's going to marry Mom.

A few years ago I attended the wedding of one of the girls who had been in the youth group Bill and I had worked with as counselors. Because she and I had always been very close she honored me by asking me to come into the bride's room to pray with her before the ceremony. Her mother and I joined her there, and after a while the rest of the wedding party began drifting in. Everyone looked splendid; the photographer came and left, and everything was ready.

The bride, radiating composure, drifted elegantly in her gown and veil that she had personally designed and sewed. "It's time to start," came the whispered words. With that, the little flower girl, already nervous and fearful, burst into tears. "I don't want to go down the aisle." Sob, sob. "I want to go home." We all stood unnerved, not knowing what to do.

Without a moment's hesitation, the bride turned to the sobbing child, dropped to her knees amid billows of white silk, and, without saying a word, put her arms out to the crying three-year-old. With tears and trembles the little girl walked right up the front of that white gown and laid her tear-stained face on that willing shoulder.

In a soft and soothing voice the bride told the sniffling tot how sad she would be if there were no pink flower petals for her to walk on. And almost before we knew it, the wedding was underway. Smiling flower girl, beautiful bride, and no evidence of shoeprints or tears — only the sweet presence of the Lord! In a time of stress the comforting touch of love had been released from one person to another.

We All Need a Touch

So many times when we need a touch, we're just too embarrassed to ask for it. I had been visiting my sister whom I rarely see, and, as she walked me to the airplane I just wanted to hug her so badly, but I didn't. I got on the plane and went home, thinking all the way, "Gosh, I wish I had hugged her." When I got home I shared it with my mom. You know what? My sister later wrote Mother a letter saying, "Gosh, I wanted to hug Mary Rae." We both missed that because both of us were too embarrassed! You see, touch puts you out on the line and makes you vulnerable, but you have to be willing to be vulnerable. I'll often just put my arms out and invite someone to a hug, and maybe they won't respond and there I stand looking foolish. But 99 times out of 100 I get the hug, and it's worth the one time that I don't. So be willing to be made vulnerable to people, so you can enjoy the benefit of the 99 rather than miss the 99 because you're afraid of being rejected that one time.

The youth man at one of the churches in which we served was always giving the guys opportunities for touch. He'd wrestle with them, play fist-a-cuffs, and do other things to give the fellows the opportunity for physical contact. They needed it and were crying for it. And if you'll admit it, you need it too. We all need to be touched.

My girls and I have something going. It started with one of my daughters when she came in one day and said, "I need a hug," and so she got a hug. So every now and then we'll say, "I need a hug." I did that just the other day. I was tired and went in to my daughter Shirlee in the kitchen and said, "I think I need a hug." I laid my head down on her shoulder and she gave me a big squeeze. Touch! Touch and go. Be generous with your affection. Never part without loving.

Go Love Again

In the Book of Hosea in the Bible we have an important teaching about love. Hosea had been instructed by God to marry a harlot because God was teaching him something about the adulterous nation of Israel. God wanted Hosea to learn what rejection felt like so he could bring an effective prophetic word to Israel. At this point Hosea was deeply hurt because of what his wife, the harlot, had done, and now the Lord tells Hosea, "Go love again" (Hosea 3:1). The word for love used in this verse is one of three important Hebrew words for love, and I want you to know what these three words are. They're not the three *Greek* love words you're thinking of—*agape, phileo,* and *eros.* These are three *Hebrew* love words.* One of them is *ahaba,* and this means affection for people and things. It can also refer to a sexual attraction. Then there's *rahamim,* which is pity for the helpless. This is a mother's love for her child. And then there's *hesed* love, and God says that this is the best love. I want to give you a definition of *hesed* love: it's the best covenant love—steadfast, kind, merciful, strong, gentle, and persevering. It carries out contractual obligations in the love relationship. That's the kind of love with which the Lord tells Hosea to love that woman again. And this is the way He tells us to love, especially in the marriage relationship. We are to love in this way, to carry out our contractual obligations even when it's rough and even when we're having trouble hanging in there.

Hesed love is the kind of love that keeps a marriage perking along when things are rotten. I talked with a woman just a while ago who had *hesed* love and hung in

* From *The New Bible Commentary, Revised* (p. 703), published by Wm. B. Eerdmans Publishing Co. Copyright © 1970 by Inter-Varsity Press, London. Used by permission.

there, and now things are getting better. *Hesed* love sticks to contractual agreements. Remember that love is not just a feeling; it's an act of giving long before it's a feeling.

I want to encourage you to get a fresh start. Begin again. Determine to have what God says is your rightful inheritance. Determine to have what He says He wants for the two of you together. Don't settle for anything less. Shoot for the goal that you've seen. Say to yourself, "That's what I want, and I'm going to get there." Settle that right now with Satan, your enemy. "Jesus and I are going this way and you can go that way. I'm not going to listen to you anymore when you tell me we can't have it better. Jesus says He's got something better for me and I'm going to get there with His help." And so you're going to walk in that way with the Lord Jesus, and it's going to get better.

Show Him You Love Him

Now for everyone's sake—for his, for yours, and for God's, love your husband and tell him you love him and demonstrate that you love him. Don't just put words there, put some action behind it and let him know that you love him, and in a way that he'll *really* know. And if he says, "You're a good wife, you're a good homemaker, and you're a good mother, but there's one area in which I wish you'd be more free with me," show him that you love him enough to be free in this area too. Move into this freedom with him and then demonstrate that freedom.

On the back cover of *Learning to Be a Woman* it

says, "A woman is not born a woman. Nor does she become one when she marries a man, bears a child and does their dirty linen. Not even when she joins a women's lib movement. A woman becomes a woman when she becomes what God wants her to be. We need to take hold of what the Bible says about femininity—that magnificent but elusive quality that every young girl yearns to develop and every older woman longs to keep."*

True Femininity

Do you know what true femininity is? It isn't just being dressed in silks or satins or being a little blonde with blue eyes. Femininity is being to your husband all that he desires, and fulfilling the call to godly womanhood. There is a variety of femininities because each of you is different, and what each of your husbands desires is different. As you fulfill those desires and respond to the desires that are his, you are very feminine.

I once counseled with a girl who thought she was very unfeminine-looking, and her husband was trying to convince her of the opposite. He found her very desirable and feminine. She was having a hard time getting over that mountain every time she looked in the mirror. And so the Lord gave us this definition of femininity: "being to your husband all that he desires, responding to and satisfying those needs and desires in him, and fulfilling the Scriptural call to godly woman-

* From *Learning to Be a Woman*, by Kenneth and Floy Smith. Copyright © 1970 by Inter-Varsity Christian Fellowship. Used by permission of InterVarsity Press, Downers Grove, Illinois 60515.

hood." That's what femininity is all about. Don't let someone tell you something else, because femininity will be different for each one of you, and you can become very, very feminine even if at this moment you think you're the most unfeminine thing on earth.

God Can Restore

God says, "They shall become one." He can heal and restore and makes things right. It can get better. He knows how to do that. He's in the business not only of repairing but of making everything new, and I hope and pray that you'll allow Him to do that. The Lord wants to do that with you. He wants to make your marriage something that you'll want to shout about from the housetops. He can make your marriage that kind of marriage. Other people will just know that the two of you have something going together, and you'll never have to say a word to anybody. It will show, because there's no way you can hide it. You see how that helps the body of Christ? You see how that helps the kids? That's what our daughter Kim said to us one day. "You and Dad have something." And it's true, we do. And though much of it came hard, now I wouldn't trade it for anything. God wants to do a unique thing with you and your husband too, so don't try to pattern it after anyone else. Let God work His special miracle for you.

O God, Bring Us the Freedom

Father, I thank you for being a God who knows everything. Nothing is hidden from You. Your eyes see everything, and You desire for each one of us to move into areas that are beyond our wildest dreams. It is Your intention that You build and repair and restore and make right, that You might bring us into a relationship that will never, never be undone by the things of the enemy or of self. You are going to cause us to walk in ways that are fulfilling and beyond the joy that we have even now. O God, You're so good to us, and we know that we ask these things in Your will because it is Your desire, and we know that if we ask what is Your will we can thank You even now, and we know that they are our present possession. You've promised that in Your Word.

Father, we pray as we link our shields of faith together. Lord, we stand against those things that would divide asunder man and wife. We stand against those things that would bring us to the threshold of divorce. We stand against those things that would separate us from the inheritance that was won for us by the shed blood of Jesus.

O Lord, take our homes, take our marriages, as we link together in faith, asking You to cause us to walk in newness of life and newness of hope. Let the light so shine, Lord, that we can't miss Your will and way. Let our hearts be tenderized before You. O God, let us be teachable and correctable. Let us walk in ways, Lord, that will bring us into the restoring love that will keep us pressing on. O God, help us. Help us meet the things that are distressing with Your love and compassion and understanding. Thank You for Your love and mercy and lovingkindness which are new every morning.

Our Father, bring us into that freedom of joy and fulfillment which is our rightful inheritance in Christ. Amen.

BIBLIOGRAPHY

Ahlem, Lloyd H., *Do I Have to Be Me?* Regal, 1973.

Augsburger, David, *Caring Enough to Confront.* Regal, 1973.

Christenson, Larry, *The Christian Family.* Bethany Fellowship, 1970.

Landorf, Joyce, *The Fragrance of Beauty.* SP Publications, 1973.

Landorf, Joyce, *Tough and Tender.* Revell, 1975.

Miles, Herbert J., *Sexual Happiness in Marriage.* Zondervan, 1967.

Morgan, Marabel, *The Total Woman.* Revell, 1973.

Narramore, Clyde M., *How to Succeed in Family Living.* Regal, 1968.

Petersen, J. Allan, and Smith, Elven and Joyce, *Two Become One,* Family Concerns, 1973.

Powell, John, *The Secret of Staying in Love.* Argus, 1974.

Scanzoni, Letha, *Sex Is a Parent Affair.* Regal, 1973.

Schaeffer, Francis A., *The Mark of the Christian.* Inter-Varsity Press, 1970.

Shedd, Charlie W., *Letters to Karen.* Abingdon, 1965.

Shedd, Charlie W., *Letters to Philip.* Revell.

Smith, Kenneth G. and Floy M., *Learning to Be a Woman*. InterVarsity Press, 1970.

Smith, Kenneth G., *Learning to Be a Man*. InterVarsity Press, 1970.

Tournier, Paul, *To Understand Each Other*. John Knox Press, 1967.

Williams, H. Page, *Do Yourself a Favor: Love Your Wife*. Logos, 1973.

Mary conducts seminars under the title *Nourishing The One* (Sexual Maturity for Women). If you would like information concerning a daylong or weekend seminar, please write to the following address:

> Mrs. Mary Detrick
> P.O. Box 20035
> San Diego, CA 92120

"JUST LIKE BEING THERE"

The content of this book is also available in tape cassette form, in a convenient protective package. You can bring the vitality and personality of great authors and speakers right into your home, car, study group or church through the magic of modern quality tape cassettes, recorded live before real audiences for your spiritual growth and listening pleasure.

You can make double use of your time too:
• listen and learn while you drive to and from work
• listen and learn while you work around your home
• listen and learn while you relax at home or on vacation

Use tape cassettes in study groups, in the church, in the home, in youth meetings. You can listen as long as you want —then stop the tape anytime while you discuss the speaker's points.